SEVEN THINGS
A LOVING

GOD
HATES

ALLEN WEBSTER

For information, please contact House to House Publishing Inc., PO Box 512, Jacksonville, AL 36265.

First Printing 2006

ISBN 978-1-933808-25-3

ATTENTION CHURCHES, UNIVERSITIES, COLLEGES, AND ORGANIZATIONS: Quantity discounts are available on bulk purchases of this book for educational and gift purposes, or as premiums for increasing magazine subscriptions or renewals. Special books or book excerpts can also be created to suit specific needs. For more information, please contact House to House Publishing Inc., PO Box 512, Jacksonville, AL 36265. Phone: 256-435-9356 www.housetohouse.com

TABLE OF CONTENTS

CHAPTER ONE

LOOKING FOR LOVE

P eople all over the world are looking for love. According to Amazon.com, there are at least 32,507 books currently in print with the word *love* in the title—more than 145,000 that deal with the subject of love. There are more than 11,000 popular albums/CDs with *love* in the title. A Google-search of the Internet reveals at least 121,000,000 websites use the word *love* as one of their key words.[1]

The Bible is a book about a love story. It is about God's love for humanity and His wooing of our affection through the Mediator, His Son. The word *love* (various forms) is found 419 times in the Bible. The greatest verse in the Bible talks of its greatest subject:

John 3:16	God's Love
For God	the greatest Being
so loved	the greatest motive
the world	the greatest number
that He gave	the greatest act
His only begotten Son	the greatest gift
that whosoever	the greatest invitation
believeth in Him	the greatest requirement
should not perish	the greatest fear
but have everlasting life	the greatest hope

Nowhere in the Bible does it say that God is hope or that God is faith, although He is the object of our hope and the source of our faith; but it does say that God is love. God's very nature is love; He invented it: "For love is of God . . . for God is love" (1 John 4:7–8). Paul chimes in: "God, who is rich in mercy, for his great love wherewith he loved us" (Ephesians 2:4). This is what sets the God of the Bible apart from all the imagined gods of heathendom—gods of war, hate, and lust. The pagans make their gods; their gods do not make them. They carry their gods; their gods do not carry them. They protect their gods; their gods do not protect them. They sacrifice to their gods; their gods do not sacrifice for them. But the true God made us, carries us, protects us, and sacrificed His Son for us.

ARE YOU LOOKING FOR LOVE THAT IS UNCONDITIONAL?

The best thing about this day is that we were showered with the love of God from morning to night. Little children sing of it, old men meditate on it, sufferers trust it, agnostics doubt it, and unbelievers scoff at it, but the love of God continues to shine with the brightness of the noonday sun.

God loves us no matter what we have done. Satan has led everyone down the wrong road (Romans 3:23). All of us have done things of which we are ashamed, or at least should be (Luke 15:15–16). Yet God still invites all to receive His love (Revelation 22:17; Matthew 11:28–30) and be saved (1 Timothy 2:4). At times it is harder for us to forgive ourselves than it is for God to forgive us. We look back over our wasted, sinful years and think, "There is no way I could ever be forgiven of that." And then God says, "I, even I, am he that blotteth out thy transgressions for mine own sake, and will not remember thy sins" (Isaiah 43:25).

When some of the very ones who had yelled in bloodthirsty hatred, "Crucify him!" later cried out in humble submission, "What must we do?" God spoke through His messenger: "Repent and be baptized everyone of you in the name of Jesus Christ for the remission of sins, and ye shall receive the gift of the Holy Ghost" (Acts 2:37–38). If God could forgive those who killed His only begotten Son, He can forgive you and me! We only need to do what He asks and then forgive ourselves.

A man named Saul (later called Paul) persecuted Christians—beating some, killing some—and made havoc of the church of Christ (Acts 7:58; 8:1; 9:1). This man learned of his sins, obeyed the Lord (Acts 9:18), and was forgiven (Acts 22:16). But he then had to learn to forgive himself. He referred to himself as "the least of all saints" (Ephesians 3:8) and the "chief of sinners," because he had been "a blasphemer, and a persecutor, and injurious" (1 Timothy 1:13, 15). He was able to put it behind him, though, and be of use to Christ.

> Brethren, I count not myself to have apprehended: but this one thing I do, forgetting those things which are behind and reaching forth unto those things which are before, I press toward the mark for the prize of the high calling of God in Christ Jesus (Philippians 3:13–14).

No matter what the old man of sin did, he can be a new creature in Christ, for when "old things are passed away; behold, all things are become new" (2 Corinthians 5:17). God has made a way of salvation for us. It is by God's grace (Ephesians 2:8), Christ's blood (Romans 5:9), and the Holy Spirit's Gospel (Romans 1:16). He requires of the sinner faith (Acts 16:31), repentance (Luke 13:3), confession (Romans 10:10), and baptism for the remission of sins (Acts 2:38; 1 Peter 3:21). After we become Christians, He commands us to remain faithful to Him (Revelation 2:10).

God loves us even when we make mistakes. Christians want to be sinless, but we are not. We make mistakes. We sometimes bring reproach on the worthy name we wear. John wrote, "If we say that we have no sin, we deceive ourselves, and the truth is not in us" (1 John 1:8). But God loves us in spite of our sins. He expects us to repent, confess, and turn from sin (Acts 8:22–24; James 5:16). Each must then forgive himself and go back to work for the Master, trying harder than ever not to sin.

God loves us even if we do not love Him. The amazing thing about God's love is that it reaches to those who do not return it.

> For when we were yet without strength, in due time Christ died for the ungodly. For scarcely for a righteous man will one die: yet peradventure for a good man some would even dare to die. But God commendeth his love toward us, in that, while we were yet sinners, Christ died for us (Romans 5:6–8).

Why would men not love God, seeing the great sacrifice He made for them? (John 3:16).

ARE YOU LOOKING FOR LOVE THAT IS PROVEN?

Love is not just something we feel; it is more often something we do. Love requires action; it is demonstrated through behavior. God's love is more than just talk; He demonstrates compassion the way He wants us to. As Paul said, "Faithful is he that calleth you, who also will do it" (1 Thessalonians 5:24). John wrote, "My little children, let us not love in word, neither in tongue; but in deed and in truth" (1 John 3:18; cf. James 2:15–16).

God demonstrates His love for us by gift-giving. One of the "five languages of love"[2] is "gift-giving." We enjoy surprising our mates with a little something we picked up on a trip. We take pleasure in giving presents to our children during the holidays. We celebrate graduations, weddings, and births with gift-giving.

God also uses this love language to express His sentiments to man. He "gave gifts unto men" (Ephesians 4:8). He leaves no one out—even His avowed enemies get daily gifts from the Creator they deny. "The Lord is good to all: and his tender mercies are over all his works" (Psalm 145:9). He gives us sunshine and rain, fruitful seasons, and beautiful vistas. Paul and Barnabas explained that God "left not himself without witness, in that he did good, and gave us rain from heaven, and fruitful seasons, filling our hearts with food and gladness" (Acts 14:17; cf. Matthew 5:45).

God demonstrates His love for us through the life of His Son. Jesus helps us to know the God of love. Various forms of the word *love* are found eighty-six times in the eighty-nine chapters of Jesus' biographies—when *compassion* is added, the total increases to one hundred times. Jesus told Philip, "If ye have seen me, ye have seen the Father" (John 14:9). We see Jesus' love demonstrated in feeding hungry people (John 6), healing hurting people (Matthew 4:24), directing lost people (Matthew 9:35–36), correcting wrong people (Matthew 23), accepting rejected people (Luke 19:1–10), and dying for lost people (Matthew 20:28).

Someone once wrote about a traveler who fell into a deep pit and couldn't get out. Several persons came along and saw him struggling in the pit.

- The sensitive person said, "I feel for you down there in that pit."
- The reflective person said, "It's logical that someone would fall into the pit."
- The aesthetic person said, "I can give you ideas on how to decorate your pit."
- The judgmental person said, "Only bad people fall into pits."
- The curious person said, "Tell me how you fell into the pit."
- The perfectionist said, "I believe you deserve your pit."
- The evaluator asked, "Are you paying taxes on this pit?"
- The self-pitying person said, "You should have seen my pit."
- The counselor said, "Just relax and don't think about the pit."
- The optimist said, "Cheer up! Things could be worse."

- The pessimist said, "Be prepared! Things will get worse."
- Jesus, seeing the man, loved him, and lifted him out of the pit.

A Christian can truthfully sing, "I was sinking deep in sin, far from the peaceful shore" when "love lifted me!"

God demonstrates His love for us through the death of His Son. The phrase "In God We Trust" first appeared on U.S. coins after April 22, 1864, when Congress passed an act authorizing the coinage of a two-cent piece bearing this motto. Thereafter, Congress extended its use to other coins. On July 30, 1956, it became the national motto. It was intended to demonstrate that our country has placed its trust in God to guide it. "The Lord recompense thy work, and a full reward be given thee of the Lord God of Israel, under whose wings thou art come to trust" (Ruth 2:12; cf. 2 Samuel 22:3; 1 Timothy 6:17).

God has an infallible track record. He can be trusted. He has proven beyond question that He loves us. The Bible says, "But God commendeth[3] [demonstrated] his love toward us, in that, while we were yet sinners, Christ died for us" (Romans 5:8).

John Griffith lived in Oklahoma in 1929, and lost all he had in the stock market crash. He moved to Mississippi where he took a job tending a bridge for a railroad trestle. One day in 1937, his eight-year-old son, Greg, spent the day with his dad at work. He played in the office that morning and asked a thousand questions. Then a ship came through and John opened the drawbridge.

Suddenly, he realized his son wasn't in the office. Frantically he looked around, and to his horror saw him climbing on the gears of the drawbridge. He hurried outside to rescue his son but just then heard what he knew was a fast-approaching passenger train, the *Memphis Express*, filled with four hundred people. He yelled to his son, but the noise of the passing ship and the oncoming train made it impossible for the boy to hear him.

John Griffith realized his horrible dilemma. If he took the time to rescue his son, the train would crash and kill all aboard. If he closed the bridge, he would sacrifice his son. He made the decision he would relive ten thousand times and pulled the lever to close the bridge. As the train went by he could see some passengers' faces. Some were reading, some waved, and all were oblivious to the sacrifice that had just been made on their behalf.

God once faced a similar dilemma. He could not save sinners and spare Jesus too. How could He be "just" and "justifier" (Romans 3:26) at the same time? God had to allow the jaws of death to close on His Son. He "spared not his own Son, but delivered him up for us all" (Romans 8:32). When sin covered the earth like white-caps cover the sea, God sent Jesus to die for you and me. "For God so loved the world, that he gave his only begotten Son, that whosoever believeth in him should not perish, but have everlasting life" (John 3:16).

Millions go by oblivious and indifferent, even some who know of the sacrifice. Still, there is one tremendous difference between the two fathers. Unlike the *Memphis Express* that caught John Griffith by surprise, sending Jesus was not a panic move. It wasn't a spontaneous decision. It was planned. Paul said, "But when the fulness of the time was come, God sent forth his Son, made of a woman, made under the law" (Galatians 4:4). Jesus' death was not the result of jealous Jews or hard-hearted Romans. It was the result of a loving God who saw there was no other way to save man. "Hereby perceive we the love of God, because he laid down his life for us" (1 John 3:16).

ARE YOU LOOKING FOR LOVE THAT AFFIRMS?

God wants us to believe in Him (John 8:24). In fact, unless we have faith in His existence, we cannot be saved (Hebrews 11:6). We have faith in God, but He also has faith in us. Sometimes He believes more in us than we believe in ourselves.

God believed in Abraham. God said of this father of the faithful: "For I know him, that he will command his children and his household after him, and they shall keep the way of the LORD, to do justice and judgment" (Genesis 18:19). Almighty God believed in Abraham enough to go out on a limb and say that his children and grand-children would be trained in the way of truth. He was right! Isaac, his son, and Jacob, his grandson, believed in God and followed in the paths of Abraham. In fact, the nation of Israel—with lapses—continued for two thousand years in the faith that once rested in their ancestor's heart.

God believed in Job. Satan suspended his pursuit of mankind long enough to report in before Jehovah (Job 1:11). "And the LORD said unto Satan, Hast thou considered my servant Job, that there is none like him in the earth, a perfect and an upright man, one that feareth God, and escheweth evil?" (Job 1:8). God issued a challenge to the old serpent by insisting he would have no success with Job. God believed in Job. He knew he would not let Him down. Job withstood the worst onslaught of devilish tor-ture recorded in the annuals of Adam's race. He did not "curse God and die," as his wife pled with him to do (Job 2:9). God believed in Job, and Job believed in God.

God believed in Rahab. Rahab was not exactly a role model for children (Joshua 2:1–6). She was the kind of person that people whispered about, pointed at, and left alone. She was a woman of loose morals and unflattering character. To put it frankly, she was a prostitute (harlot, Hebrews 11:31; James 2:25). She sold her body to men who passed through her city and stayed at her inn. During these pagan times, harlotry was often a part of worship.

Rahab was also a traitor. She betrayed her country by harboring its enemies. Rahab was a liar. She said the spies had left, when they were hiding on her roof. Some use this as an example of situation ethics (cf. Romans 3:8), but God never approves of lying (Proverbs 6:17; Ephesians 4:25). He could have protected the spies in a way that did not require sin. Rahab was accepted in spite of her lie, not because of it.

Other Bible characters are complimented, though guilty of serious sins (e.g., David committed adultery, 2 Samuel 11). Many of those who are commended in Hebrews 11 are not praised for all they did (Abraham lied; Noah got drunk; Samson slept around). They are praised simply for some heroic act of faith. We may heartily commend an orator for eloquence while earnestly opposing an idea he advanced. Being a Canaanite, Rahab may not have been taught that lying was evil.

In spite of her sins, God believed in Rahab. He pardoned her iniquity. He was willing to forget her previous life and forgive her falsehood regarding the spies. He saw something good in her. He believed she had changed and that there was something worthwhile about her. God liked her faith and her works. In Hebrews 11 she is eulogized for her faith, and in James 2 she is complimented for her works. Remarkably, Rahab is even listed in the genealogy of God's Son (Matthew 1:5). God allowed this formerly loose woman to marry into Israel—His holy people—and become the mother of a child. Some writers speculate that her husband Salmon was one of the spies whom she befriended; if so, what a beautiful love story! Rahab became a princess in Israel; more important, she became a part of the ancestral line that ran from Abraham through King David to Jesus Christ.

Incidentally, in giving the Lord's genealogy, Matthew mentions only four women—Tamar, Rahab, Ruth, and, implicitly, Bathsheba. Three of these have tainted names. Most people would be embarrassed to have harlots and adulteresses in their family tree. If it had been in their power, they would never have allowed them to have been there in the first place. It was within God's power, but He believed in Rahab to the point that He put her in His family album!

God believed in Peter. Peter cursed and swore that He did not know Jesus of Nazareth. After Jesus had been his friend, after He had taught him for three years, even after Peter had boasted that he would die before he would deny, Peter blushed at a maiden's question. He pretended he had never met Jesus and backed that affirmation with profanity, which always disassociates one from Christ. Afterward, Peter wept like a scolded child. He was sorry for his failure. God could have given up on Peter. He could have found someone else to be the apostle to the circumcision, but God still believed in Peter. And when it came time to pick somebody to be the head spokesman for Christ on the inauguration of the kingdom, God tapped Peter to deliver the stirring speech that launched the Gospel dispensation (Acts 2).

God believed in Saul. Acts 9:15 tells us God believed in Saul: "The Lord said . . . he is a chosen vessel unto me, to bear my name before the Gentiles, and kings, and the children of Israel." Everybody else saw the church's worst enemy; God saw its greatest promoter. Others saw one who could dish out persecution; God saw one who could take it. They saw a blasphemer; God saw a preacher. They saw a murderer; God saw a missionary.

These instances show that sometimes God believes in us when others, or even we ourselves, don't. Those who faithfully serve and suffer for Him He will not only protect, but prefer, and will do for them more than they can ask or think (Ephesians 3:20). God can use people who have made mistakes. We read of publicans and harlots entering into the kingdom, and not just tolerated, but welcomed (Matthew 21:31). Those on Pentecost had killed Jesus, but they became the first Christians (Acts 2:22, 41). The Corinthians had been immoral, but God forgave them (1 Corinthians 6:9–11). Believe in God. Let God believe in you.

ARE YOU LOOKING FOR LOVE THAT LASTS?

Many of us have loved and lost. In a weak moment we can still feel the pain of being jilted by a college sweetheart who had promised undying love. We've cried when a husband left for another woman, or put a fist through the wall when a wife found someone at work "who understood her." We've lost countless nights of sleep over a child who turned against us, even though we did everything in our power to help him or her.

Are you ready for love that lasts? Then get to know God. Both the Old and New Testaments talk of the eternal nature of God's affection. "The LORD hath appeared of old unto me, saying, yea, I have loved thee with an everlasting love: therefore with lovingkindness have I drawn thee" (Jeremiah 31:3). In 2 Thessalonians 2:16 Paul tells us that both God and Jesus have provided love and "everlasting consolation and good hope through grace," demonstrating that God's love cannot be measured by time.

God's love reaches into the eternal past. Moses said, "LORD, thou hast been our dwelling place in all generations. Before the mountains were brought forth, or ever thou hadst formed the earth and the world, even from everlasting to everlasting, thou art God" (Psalm 90:1–2). John added, "And all that dwell on the earth shall worship him, every one whose name hath not been written from the foundation of the world in the book of life of the Lamb that hath been slain" (Revelation 13:8). Jesus mentioned this truth, as well: "Then shall the King say unto them on his right hand, Come, ye blessed of my Father, inherit the kingdom prepared for you from the foundation of the world" (Matthew 25:34).

God's love continues in the present. Peter wrote, "The Lord is not slack concerning his promise, as some men count slackness; but is longsuffering to us-ward, not willing that any should perish, but that all should come to repentance" (2 Peter 3:9).

God's love reaches into the eternal future. How long will God love us? Forever! When God told Israel in Jeremiah 31:3 that He loved them "with an everlasting love" He implied that it went just as far into the future as it went into the past. Jesus loved His disciples "unto the end" (John 13:1). He promised to go with us "to the end of the world" (Matthew 28:20) and to "confirm you unto the end, that ye may be blameless in the day of our Lord Jesus Christ" (1 Corinthians 1:8). The duration of God's love is demonstrated in the *Parable of the Prodigal Son* (Luke 15:11–24). God's love will last so long that nothing can separate us from it (Romans 8:38–39).

In Ephesians 3:10–11, we observe the length of God's love (*aion,* eternal, "for ever, an unbroken age, perpetuity of time, eternity"; Ephesians 1:4; 2 Timothy 1:9). When the Lord purposes something, it comes to pass (cf. Isaiah 14:24, 27; 46:10–11; Jeremiah 51:29; Romans 8:28–30). His love will be there to the end, but we must continue to seek for it (Hebrews 3:6, 14; 6:11; 1 Peter 1:13). John wrote of what awaits us: "For the Lamb that is in the midst of the throng shall be their shepherd, and shall guide them unto fountains of waters of life: and God shall wipe away every tear from their eyes" (Revelation 7:17).

Since people are looking for love, and "God is love" (1 John 4:8), then God is what people are looking for!

Questions to Consider and Discuss:

1. What is often called the greatest verse of the Bible? Please list the great things it mentions phrase by phrase.
2. Choose one of the following statements for further discussion.
   a. At times it is harder for us to forgive ourselves than it is for God to forgive us.
   b. The pagans carry their gods; their gods do not carry them.
   c. If God could forgive those who killed His only begotten Son, He can forgive you and me!
   d. "I was sinking deep in sin, far from the peaceful shore" when "love lifted me!"
   e. God has an infallible track record.
   f. When sin covered the earth like whitecaps cover the sea, God sent Jesus to die for you and me.
   g. We have faith in God, but God also has faith in us.
   h. Everybody else saw in Saul the church's worst enemy; God saw its greatest promoter.
   i. Publicans and harlots entering into the kingdom were not just tolerated, they were welcomed (Matthew 21:31).
3. What steps are involved in becoming a Christian? What Scriptures give these commands?
4. Does the statement "God loves us in spite of our sins" give us license to sin? (Romans 6:1).
5. Give some examples from Jesus' life and from your love for your family of how love is not just something we feel; it is more often something we do.
6. Do you agree that "In God We Trust" belongs on our currency and in a prominent place in society? Why or why not?
7. Explain God's dilemma involving being both "just" and "justifier" (cf. Romans 3:23–26) at the same time. How did He accomplish it?
8. Give some examples of how God believes in man.
9. Does Rahab's lie show that it is permissible to lie under some circumstances?
10. Explain how you would answer someone who doesn't believe a loving God could send anyone to eternal punishment.

CHAPTER TWO

A PROUD LOOK

Proverbs 6:17

When Cassius Clay was in his prime, he was known for his "float like a butterfly, sting like a bee, I'm the greatest. I'm Mohammed Ali" boast. Once when he was about to take off on an airplane flight, the stewardess reminded him to fasten his seat belt. He said brashly, "Superman don't need no seat belt." The stewardess quickly came back, "Superman don't need no airplane, either." Ali fastened his belt.[1]

Truly, "the rod hath blossomed, pride hath budded" (Ezekiel 7:10) in each human heart. It still flowers, blooms, and blossoms in most hearts today. The word *pride* (in various forms) appears more than a hundred times in Scripture.[2]

EARS, EYES, HEARTS, AND HEADS

One New Testament word for pride[3] means "to envelop with smoke; to inflate with self-conceit; be high-minded." A missionary once told how he found it hard to translate the concept of pride to one tribe. He finally decided to use their words for the "ears being too far apart." An "inflated head" may be hard to improve on as a meaning for pride. On the other hand, *humble* is defined as "a state or quality of being humble in spirit; freedom from pride or arrogance."[4] It signifies "low-lying; on the ground; being brought low."[5] It is similar to the Bible word *abase* (Matthew 23:12).

The first thing that God hates is "a proud look" (Proverbs 6:17). Martin Luther observed, "God creates out of nothing. Therefore, until a man is nothing, God can make nothing out of him."[6] The phrase "a proud look" is literally "eyes of loftiness." David mentioned "the pride of his countenance" (Psalm 10:4; cf. 18:27; Isaiah 2:11). He guarded his eyes from haughtiness: "LORD, my heart is not haughty, nor mine eyes lofty: neither do I exercise myself in great matters, or in things too high for me" (Psalm 131:1). In his kingdom, David condemned pride: "Whoso privily slandereth his neighbour, him will I cut off: him that hath an high look and a proud heart will not I suffer" (Psalm 101:5). Agur later spoke of this idea again: "There is a generation, O how lofty are their eyes! and their eyelids are lifted up" (Proverbs 30:13). Jesus mentioned "pride" and "an evil eye" together (Mark 7:20–23). We use a similar expression when we speak of a person "looking down his nose" at someone else. In 2 Timothy 3:2, the word translated *proud*[7] means "appearing above others (conspicuous), i.e. haughty."

UNLUCKY 13

Pride is condemned at least thirteen times in the book of Proverbs:

- "The fear of the LORD is to hate evil: pride, and arrogancy, and the evil way, and the froward mouth, do I hate" (8:13).

- "When pride cometh, then cometh shame: but with the lowly is wisdom" (11:2). Someone observed, "Pride is the only disease that everyone around you suffers from, except yourself." Two Texans were trying to impress each other with the size of their ranches. One asked the other, "What's the name of your ranch?" He replied, "The Rocking R, ABC, Flying W, Circle C, Bar U, Staple Four, Box D, Rolling M, Rainbow's End, Silver Spur Ranch." The questioner was much impressed and exclaimed, "Whew! That's sure some name! How many head of cattle do you run?" The rancher answered, "Not many. Very few survive the branding."[8]

- "Only by pride cometh contention: but with the well advised is wisdom" (13:10).

- "In the mouth of the foolish is a rod of pride: but the lips of the wise shall preserve them" (14:3).

- "The LORD will destroy the house of the proud: but he will establish the border of the widow" (15:25).

- "Every one that is proud in heart is an abomination to the LORD: though hand join in hand, he shall not be unpunished" (16:5).

- "Pride goeth before destruction, and a haughty spirit before a fall" (16:18).

- "Better it is to be of an humble spirit with the lowly, than to divide the spoil with the proud" (16:19).

- "An high look, and a proud heart, and the plowing of the wicked, is sin" (21:4).

- "Proud and haughty scorner is his name, who dealeth in proud wrath" (21:24).

- "He that is of a proud heart stirreth up strife: but he that putteth his trust in the LORD shall be made fat" (28:25).

- "A man's pride shall bring him low: but honour shall uphold the humble in spirit" (29:23). Someone said, "People are strange: they want the front of the bus, the back of the church, and the center of attention."[9] Another observed, "A sure cure for conceit and pride is a visit to the cemetery, where eggheads and boneheads get equal billing."[10]

BIG-TIME CONSEQUENCES FOR SUCH A SMALL-TIME SIN

Most view pride as a small sin, if a sin at all, but God sees it as a major infraction. Our thoughts are not His thoughts (Isaiah 55:8), nor our judgments as wise as His. Since pride is number one on God's hate list (Proverbs 6:16–17), He puts it ahead of such sins as murder, adultery, and drunkenness. Pride was the first overt act of sin in heaven—the original sin (cf. 1 Timothy 3:6). Satan cast his evil gaze on the throne of God and planned to occupy that seat himself. Later he came to man in the Garden of Eden and used pride to lure Eve into the first human sin. His sales pitch was, "Ye shall be as gods . . . " (Genesis 3:5). By contrast, Jesus was never proud (Matthew 11:29; Philippians 2:5; 1 Peter 2:21–22); He urged all His followers to be humble (Matthew 5:3).

God affixes some hefty punishments to this "light-weight" offense.

Pride condemns nations and destroys kings. John Adams said,

> Whenever vanity and gaiety, a love of pomp and dress . . . expensive diversions and elegant entertainments, get the better of principles and judgments of men and

women, there is no knowing where they will stop, nor into what evils—natural, moral, or political—they will lead us."[11]

Pride was the sin of Judah (Jeremiah 13:9), Moab (Jeremiah 48:29), Babylon (Jeremiah 50:29), Sodom (Ezekiel 16:49), Egypt (Ezekiel 30:6), Israel (Hosea 5:5), Edom (Obadiah 1:3), Philistia (Zechariah 9:6), and Assyria (Zechariah 10:11). It is said that when a victorious Roman general arrived back in Rome, he was given a hero's welcome and a triumphant parade of victory, but a philosopher was also hired to ride beside him in the victory parade. As the victor acknowledged the cheers of the crowd, the philosopher kept whispering in his ear: "You are mortal. You are mortal."

Pride defiles individuals. Jesus said,

> That which cometh out of the man, that defileth the man. For from within, out of the heart of men, proceed evil thoughts, adulteries, fornications, murders, thefts, covetousness, wickedness, deceit, lasciviousness, an evil eye, blasphemy, pride, foolishness:[12] all these evil things come from within, and defile the man (Mark 7:20–23).

Noting the downward progression in which pride leads one, Ben Franklin said, "Pride breakfasted with plenty, dined with poverty, and supped with infamy." Perhaps no one illustrates the foolish extremes to which pride will go better than Simon in the story of Lucian. He was so proud of his high station in life that he set fire to the house in which he was born. He was afraid someone would point out his humble birthplace![13]

Pride can destroy novice[14] elders and unwary preachers (Romans 16:17–18; 1 Timothy 3:6). Even in the church, leaders may be tempted by pride. Jesus put it this way: "And whosoever of you will be the chiefest, shall be servant of all" (Mark 10:44; cf. Matthew 20:26–27). D. L. Moody stated it memorably: "Be humble or you'll stumble." God's shepherds should readily agree with Goethe: "The deed is everything, the glory nothing." Someone wisely observed: "Once the game is over, the king and the pawn go back into the same box."

Pride is a downhill road to a fiery crash. Pride is one of the three avenues along which all sin passes. John wrote, "For all that is in the world, the lust of the flesh, and the lust of the eyes, and the pride of life, is not of the Father, but is of the world" (1 John 2:16). Pride has been the basis of many sins from the Garden of Eden—"make thee wise"— to tomorrow's headlines. Paul lists the proud with the vilest of sinners (Romans 1:30; 2 Timothy 3:2).

SINS LINKED TO PRIDE IN THE BIBLE

Pride is the canal through which many sins flow, the snowball that starts an avalanche of iniquity, or the tremor that ends up on God's Richter scale. Conceit is the genesis of many sins.

- Pride caused some to get hung up on—dote over—useless questions (1 Timothy 6:4–5).
- Pride caused people to falsely accuse/judge others' motives (1 Samuel 17:28).
- Pride caused some to forge lies (Psalm 119:69).
- Pride caused some to deal perversely (unfairly) with others (Psalm 119:78); dig pits for others (Psalm 119:85; 140:5); oppress others (Psalm 119:122; cf. 10:2).
- Pride caused some to stir up strife (Proverbs 13:10; 28:25).

Pride caused men to refuse to seek after God (Psalm 10:4; 2 Thessalonians 2:3). A disciple once asked Socrates, "Why is it, sir, that you tell everyone who wants to become your disciple to look into this pond and tell you what he sees?"

"That is very simple, my friend," he answered. "I am ready to accept all those who tell me they see fish swimming around. But those who see only their own image mirrored in the water are in love with their own ego. I have no use for them."

God has no use for the proud, either. Certainly He is no respecter of persons (Acts 10:34; Romans 2:11), and will require the same of each person at the Judgment. Someone asked an insightful question: "Why does everyone think he is an exception to the rules?"

Pride caused some to refuse to get their hands dirty. The proud nobles would not help Nehemiah rebuild the wall (Nehemiah 3:5). Small men in big places have often taken the hands-off approach to work projects. A rider on horseback, many years ago, came across a squad of soldiers trying to move a heavy piece of timber. A corporal was giving loud orders to "heave." But the timber was too heavy for the squad. "Why don't you help them?" asked the quiet man on the horse, addressing the important corporal.

"Me? Why, I'm a corporal!"

Dismounting, the stranger took his place with the soldiers. "Now, all together, boys, heave!" he said. And the big piece of timber fell into place. The stranger remounted and addressed the corporal: "The next time you have a piece of timber too big for your men to handle, corporal, send for the commander-in-chief." The horseman was George Washington. We are not greater than our Master (John 13:16), either. He was willing to get His hands dirty—and so must we be.

Pride caused some to boast and make inappropriate statements (Psalm 12:4; 1 Samuel 2:3; Proverbs 14:3). No one can glorify himself and Christ at the same time. He who had every reason to be proud did not seek His own glory (John 8:54). Jesus was born in a manger, washed His disciples' feet, and died stripped and shamed (Philippians 2:5–8). Yet human nature is different. One fisherman observed: "No man having caught a large fish goes home through the alley."

On May 31, 1889, a terrible flood at Johnstown, Pennsylvania, took thousands of lives. One survivor told people about the flood every chance he got. The story goes that he died and went to heaven, where he was told he could have anything he wanted. He said he wanted a great hall where he could tell his story to tens of thousands. The day came and the hall was packed. As he was ready to make his talk about the Johnstown flood, the master of ceremonies told him he would be the second speaker on the program. He would be preceded by a man named Noah![15]

Remember: "Don't brag—it isn't the whistle that pulls the train." The Academy Awards presented a special award posthumously to Irving G. Thalberg. Thalberg was a genius producer of the '20s and '30s who died at age thirty-seven. His excellent work made a lasting difference in the film industry. What is noteworthy was that he never allowed his name to appear on the credits of any of his films. "Self-praise is not worth having," was his attitude. Since Ephesians 4:2 puts "lowliness" first, as the basis and precursor of all other graces, it makes sense that haughtiness would be the foundation of all houses built on the sand.

Pride caused some to scorn others and hold them in derision (Psalm 119:51, 122; Galatians 2:12; James 2:1–6; 4:6, 10). Pride keeps us from obeying Paul's directive: "Be of the same mind one toward another. Mind not high things, but condescend to men of low estate. Be not wise in your own conceits" (Romans 12:16). The state of Illinois gets its name from an Indian word to which a French suffix was added. It means "tribe of superior men." Certainly modern-day residents of Illinois do not ordinarily boast of themselves as superior men, yet throughout history there have been those who have. In Nazi Germany, for example, Adolph Hitler taught his people that they were a superior race.[16]

None of us really has a right to look down our noses at others. Alexander the Great, seeing Diogenes looking attentively at a parcel of human bones, asked the philosopher what he was looking for. Diogenes replied: "That which I cannot find—the difference between your father's bones and those of his slaves."[17] A bubble appears bigger than a water drop, but it is not. It is just a "puffed up" drop of water—H_2O that's full of air. Some people are like bubbles. The "I'm-glad-I'm-not-like-him" attitude of the Pharisee in Jesus' story (Luke 18:11) must never make its home in our hearts, much less pass through the gates of our mouths. It is never good for one to brag about how good one is, especially in a prayer! God knows the truth. God is the only one in a position to look down on anyone.

Pride caused some to oppose God's Word (Jeremiah 43:2; John 8:30–45). In *Paradise Lost*, Milton demonstrated Satan's prideful attitude by having him say, "Better to reign in hell than serve in heaven." Many today live these words but would not dare say them.

Pride caused some to harden the mind and refuse to repent (Daniel 5:20). We must be willing to humbly submit to God's commands (Acts 2:38; 22:16), and admit error and repent when necessary (Acts 8:22). Any of us can fall from grace, and most of us have—at least temporarily. Paul admonished: "Wherefore let him that thinketh he standeth take heed lest he fall" (1 Corinthians 10:12). The test comes when we realize we have taken a wrong path. Will we admit it? Will we come back? Or will we harden our conscience? For contrast, consider David's soft conscience after he cut off Saul's skirt in the cave at Engedi. "David's heart smote him" (1 Samuel 24:5). Much later in life, he still had enough conscience left to be bothered when he sinned in numbering Israel (2 Samuel 24:10).

Pride caused some to deceive themselves (Obadiah 1:3). "People who sing their own praises do so without accompaniment." When success comes our way, there is usually someone around to help us maintain perspective. TV newsman Tom Brokaw tells a story on himself that illustrates this point. Brokaw was wandering through Bloomingdale's in New York one day, shortly after he was promoted to co-host the *Today Show*. That show was a pinnacle of sorts for Brokaw after years of work, first in Omaha, then for NBC in Los Angeles and Washington, and he was feeling good about himself. He noticed a man who kept looking at him. Finally, the man approached him, and Brokaw was sure he was about to reap the first fruits of being a New York television celebrity. The man pointed his finger and said, "Tom Brokaw, right?"

"Right."

"You used to do the morning news on KMTV in Omaha, right?"

"That's right," said Brokaw, getting set for the accolades to follow.

"I knew it the minute I spotted you," the fellow said. Then he paused and added, "Whatever happened to you?"[18]

Pride caused some to oppose elders (1 Peter 5:5). Regarding our attitude toward elders, the Holy Spirit said, "Obey them that have the rule over you, and submit yourselves:

for they watch for your souls, as they that must give account, that they may do it with joy, and not with grief: for that is unprofitable for you" (Hebrews 13:17).

HOW LOW CAN YOU GO?

God keeps His distance from the proud (Psalm 138:6). He said to Job out of a whirl-wind: "Look on every one that is proud, and bring him low; and tread down the wicked in their place" (Job 40:12). He just cannot stomach—suffer—a high look or a proud heart (Psalm 101:5). He resists and abases (James 4:6; Matthew 23:12) proud people. He even threatens them: "I will cause the arrogancy of the proud to cease, and will lay low the haughtiness of the terrible" (Isaiah 13:11; cf. Malachi 4:1). Nebuchadnezzar learned the hard way that God makes no idle threats. After God took him down several notches, this humbled king said, "[I will] praise and extol and hon-our the King of heaven, all whose works are truth, and his ways judgment: and those that walk in pride he is able to abase" (Daniel 4:37; cf. 5:20–24).

Conversely, God accepts and defends the humble: "To this man will I look, even to him that is poor and of a contrite spirit, and trembleth at my word" (Isaiah 66:2). Jesus said, "Blessed are the poor in spirit: for theirs is the kingdom of heaven" (Matthew 5:3; cf. 20:20–28). He promised, "He that shall humble himself shall be exalted" (Matthew 23:12). If we are willing to come to God on that basis, God will receive us with grace. The Lord's half-brother and whole-hearted follower said: "But he giveth more grace. Wherefore he saith, God resisteth the proud, but giveth grace unto the humble" (James 4:6).

"Hear ye, and give ear; be not proud: for the LORD hath spoken"
(Jeremiah 13:15).

Questions to Consider and Discuss:

1. Why do you think that a proud look leads God's list of hated things?

2. What are the three avenues along which all sin passes? (1 John 2:16). Give an example from this week's news reports that illustrates each one.

3. How do you remind yourself to keep a proper perspective when tempted to be proud? List specific guidelines.

4. What Bible characters illustrate the truth, "When pride cometh, then cometh shame"? (Proverbs 11:2). What famous people come to mind as having learned this lesson the hard way?

5. Which one of the following statements strikes a chord with you? Comment briefly on it:
   a. No one can glorify self and Christ at the same time.
   b. Pride is the only disease that everyone around you suffers from, except yourself.
   c. No man having caught a large fish goes home through the alley.
   d. Be humble or you'll stumble.

6. In what ways can we help our children or grandchildren be humble, but also self-assured? How can good self-esteem and humility coexist?

7. How do you think the emphasis on pride in schools, sports, and society influences Christians?

8. How did Satan use pride in seducing Eve and tempting Jesus?

9. How can we help others overcome their pride and submit to the Gospel of Christ?

10. In what ways do you think God keeps His promise in James 4:6 to resist the proud, and give grace to the humble?

CHAPTER THREE

A LYING TONGUE

L ying, the second thing God hates, is a common sin. Groucho Marx said, "There is one way to find out if a man is honest—ask him. If he says yes, you know he is crooked." The abuse of the tongue is something that is common to all races and all languages.

The psalmist, probably David, overstated it a bit when he said, "I said in my haste, All men are liars" (Psalm 116:11). Still, there may be more lying going on than we have considered. "If you ask the average person, 'Do you lie?' they would say, 'No, I never lie,' or they might say, 'Oh, occasionally a white lie,'" says Robert Feldman, a social psychologist at the University of Massachusetts. "But if you look at your own behavior over the course of a day, you'll find a very different story." Many people's internal lie detectors need a tune-up. Consider these statements:[1]

- In *The Day America Told the Truth* it is related that 91 percent of those surveyed lie routinely about matters they consider trivial, 36 percent lie about important matters; 86 percent lie regularly to parents, 75 percent to friends, 73 percent to siblings, and 69 percent to spouses.[2]
- Most people lie to others once or twice a day and deceive about 30 people per week.
- According to Dr. Michael Lewis of the Robert Wood Johnson Medical School in New Jersey, "In a single day, most of us lie . . . a minimum of 25 times."
- The average is seven times per hour if you count the times people lie to themselves.[3]

- People lie in 30 to 38 percent of all their interactions, including interactions with relatives. Of those who admitted lying, 70 percent said they would do it again.[4]
- In a survey of college students, 95 percent were willing to tell at least one lie to a potential employer to win a job, and 41 percent had already done so.
- Human beings, according to psychologist Jerald Jellison of the University of Southern California, are lied to about 200 times a day, roughly one untruth every five minutes.[5]

WHO LIES?

As a rule,

- men lie more than women,
- young men lie more than older men, and
- unemployed people lie more than those with jobs.[6]

Studies reveal that socially skillful people tell more lies than people who are socially unskilled.[7] Children with lower IQs tell the truth more often than healthy, intelligent, well-adjusted kids who learn to lie. Knowing "when it is appropriate to lie" and "bend the truth" is part of a broad array of social skills. Studies show that children who are the most believable liars tend to have a lot of friends and become the "leader of the pack."

WHAT ARE THE DIFFERENT KINDS OF LIES?

Some have used creative words to explain away lying. Alexander Haig said, "That's not a lie; it's a terminological inexactitude. Also, a tactical misrepresentation." Abraham Lincoln's famous quotation fits such redefining: "How many legs does a dog have if you call the tail a leg? Four. Calling a tail a leg doesn't make it a leg." We know a lie is an untruth. It is something told to deceive. But there are kinds of lies that may not be as easily recognized—remember that all lying is condemned, according to Revelation 21:8. An unknown author has compiled the following list:

- **Twisting words:** Making a person say something he did not say.
- **Twisting truth:** Clever wording to make a lie out of a fact. Falsehoods were told on Christ both before His death (Matthew 26:61), and after (Matthew 28:13–15).
- **Shading the truth:** A perversion of the facts.
- **Half-truths:** Part of the truth, disguised as the whole truth. Morally, it is significant that the court demands of each witness that he "tell the truth, the

whole truth, and nothing but the truth." Someone observed that a half-truth is often a lot less than that. Abraham told a half-truth about Sarah being his sister—she was his half sister—but it was a whole lie because they did not live together as brother and sister (Genesis 12:13; 20:2).

- **Misstatement of fact:** Just a plain, unvarnished lie. Satan added only one word to God's statement, but completely changed God's intent (Genesis 3:4).
- **Jumping to a conclusion:** Assuming one knows when one does not.
- **Crafty questions:** Creating a doubt and unwarranted suspicion.
- **Bodily movement:** A wink, a nod, a smile conveying deception (cf. Proverbs 6:12–14).
- **Slandering:** Uttering false charges which damage a reputation.
- **Gossiping:** Indulging in sensational, intimate chatter.
- **Judging:** Arriving at a verdict of guilty, without all the facts (cf. Matthew 7:1–2).
- **Exaggerating:** Enlarging a thing beyond the bounds of truth.
- **Presuming:** Accusation backed up by probability instead of facts.
- **Accusations:** Condemning a person on purely circumstantial evidence.
- **Insinuations:** Making statements which leave untrue impressions.
- **Inference:** A chain of reasoning which condemns without evidence.
- **Innuendo:** A veiled reflection on one's character or reputation.
- **Surmises:** Placing guilt when the evidence is scanty or slight.
- **Suspicion:** Casting a cloud of mistrust without evidence.
- **Silence:** Withholding information which could clear the "guilty" one.
- **Flattery:** Insincere and excessive praise from motives of self-interest.
- **Quotation:** Making another person do your lying for you.
- **White lies:** Just plain black lies a hypocrite has tried to whitewash.

What about "little white lies"? White lies are the most common form of duplicity. They are part of a large number of lies often regarded as so trivial that they are grouped together and considered acceptable. Someone compiled the following list:

- Lies told on the spur of the moment, for lack of reflection, or to get out of a scrape.
- Lies told to boast or exaggerate self, or to depreciate and understate others.
- Lies told or repeated in gossip.
- Lies told in order to simply say something or to pass the time (cf. "every idle word," Matthew 12:36–37).
- The substitution of a quick lie for a lengthy explanation one might otherwise have to provide for something not worth spending time on.

All lying is wrong! Why? *First, what a liar perceives as harmless or even beneficial may not be seen by the deceived in the same way.*

Second, the failure to look at an entire practice rather than at one's own isolated case blinds liars to the cumulative harm of deceptive activities.

Third, telling lies is addictive. Some tell a few white lies; others tell more. The indiscriminate use of such lies can lead to greater deception. The first lie requires a second to cover it up, then a third, and so on, until the liar loses track. Thomas Jefferson said,

> He who permits himself to tell a lie once, finds it much easier to do it a second and third time, till at length it becomes habitual; he tells lies without attending to it, and truth without the world's believing him. This falsehood of the tongue leads to that of the heart, and in time depraves all its good dispositions.

Steven Soderbergh said, "Lying is like alcoholism. You are always recovering" (cf. James 3:8). Mark Twain said, "If you tell the truth, you don't have to remember anything." The aggregate harm from a large number of white lies is highly undesirable for a liar, for those deceived, and for society in general.

Fourth, the combined and long-term effects of deception are far-reaching. Disagreeable facts that are sugarcoated—the sad news that is softened or denied altogether—are eventually going to be known. Some lie to children or to the ill about important matters such as birth, death, adoption, and divorce. Should parents who have adopted a child pretend that they are his biological parents? Should parents say, "Mommy and Daddy are going to live apart awhile," knowing that a divorce is permanent? Should critically ill wives or husbands, afraid of their mate's inability to cope, lie to them about their condition? An adopted child will sooner or later know the truth. Ill patients, or their mates, will eventually know the truth, and they may have some spiritual matters they need to take care of before it is too late (cf. 2 Kings 20:1).

Telling a lie is always wrong. Sometimes, however, people can be cruel in telling the truth. Discretion and respect for the privacy of others must also govern what is spoken (Matthew 7:12). Even if unfavorable reports are true, is it right to say something that injures another? Why not leave a hurtful thing unsaid? Why tell a general white lie about a gift, a kind act, or a newborn baby when one can make a different truthful statement? A little white lie is just as sinful as a big black lie—exaggerating, misleading, deceiving—but a compliment on another subject is right and loving.

Specific liars mentioned in the Bible include the following:

- A man who adds to God's Word is a liar (Proverbs 30:6; cf. Romans 3:4). The Bible describes the man of sin, or antichrist, as a liar (2 Thessalonians 2:9–10). There were prophets in the Old Testament who prophesied lies and were dreamers of false dreams (Jeremiah 5:31; 29:9). Religious frauds are the worst liars because false doctrine destroys the souls of men (2 Thessalonians 2:11–12; 1 John 4:1; 1 Thessalonians 5:21; Revelation 2:2–3).
- One who says that he has not sinned is a liar (1 John 1:8–10).
- One who says, "I know God" but does not obey Him, is a liar (1 John 2:4).
- One who denies Christ is a liar (1 John 2:22).
- One who says he loves God but hates his brother is a liar (1 John 4:20–21).

TO WHOM ARE LIES TOLD?

Children lie to parents. David wrote, "The wicked are estranged from the womb: they go astray as soon as they be born, speaking lies" (Psalm 58:3). This can be verified by each mother and dad. Eighty-six percent of teens lie to parents; college students lie in 50 percent of conversations with their mothers. The duties to honor, respect, and obey parents (Ephesians 6:1–3) forbid lying to them.

Boyfriends lie to girlfriends—and vice versa. In one survey, 100 percent of dating couples lied to each other in about a third of their conversations. Relationships built on lies are insecure. Trust is the basis of marriage, and lies destroy trust. In fact, lying is the number one reason that people lose trust.[8]

Citizens lie to the government—and vice versa. According to the U.S. government, more than ten million working Americans are less than completely honest and revealing when they file their tax returns, "to the tune of a $200 billion annual loss to the government." We are to render "tribute to whom tribute" is due (Romans 13:6–7). Governments also lie to citizens and to other governments. Someone reasoned, "What is diplomacy, for the most part, but the art of lying?"

Employees lie to employers. From 35 to 80 percent of resumes contain lies, according to one company which screens applications for employers.[9] "The Liars Index, a semiannual survey conducted by Jude M. Werra & Associates, a Wisconsin-based executive search firm, found that about one in every seven executive candidates lies about his credentials. Resume puffery can take many forms, but the most common is the claim of a degree that was not earned—35.9 percent of liars made that claim."[10]

Further, 20 to 30 percent of middle managers surveyed had written fraudulent internal reports.

Recipients lie to insurance companies. Seventy percent of doctors believe it is ethical to deceive health insurance companies when they submit bills. Stealing by telling a lie is just as wrong as stealing with a gun (Ephesians 4:28).

Lawyers lie in courts. In some cases, attorneys aren't supposed to present the truth; their job is to advance their clients' cases. To assist a guilty criminal to go free is little different from driving a getaway car.

Students lie to teachers. Is a student's grade in school or college a mark of knowledge and work or a tribute to deceit?

> The Center for Academic Integrity (CAI) reports that: On most university campuses more than 75 percent of students admit to some cheating. About one-third of 2,100 participating students in a . . . survey on 21 university campuses nationwide admitted to "serious test cheating." Half of the students in that survey admitted to "one or more instances of serious cheating on written assignments." The Center for Academic Integrity reports research on nearly 4,500 high school students in 25 schools. . . . Seventy-four percent admitted to "serious test cheating," 72 percent to "serious cheating on written assignments." Over half admitted to some form of Internet plagiarism.[11]

Preachers lie to members. The old prophet introduced in 1 Kings 13:11 is an example of lying in the name of the Lord.[12] He lived in Bethel, and when Jeroboam set up a false altar there, the old prophet's sons went to the dedication. His sons came home excited because a young prophet from neighboring Judah had also come. He had denounced the king, the false priests, and the altar. He had miraculously paralyzed the king's arm, and then had healed him when the king pled for mercy. Then the king had invited the prophet to eat at the palace. The prophet refused, saying that God forbade him to eat with anyone at Bethel. This news excited the old prophet. Perhaps moved with envy against the successful young prophet, he resorted to deception. He found the young prophet and invited him to come home for the night.

The young man refused, explaining that God would not allow it. Then the wicked old man pretended to have received an additional message from God. You can almost hear his flattery, "We are on the same side; we are brothers in the faith. Besides, my boys are eager to meet you. They were tremendously impressed with you today." Thus the deceiver laid siege to the young man's heart: "But he lied unto him," comments the Holy Spirit (1 Kings 13:18). Perhaps the young man was hungry and tired. Whatever the reason, he yielded. The consequence was his early grave (1 Kings 13:22–24). The old prophet buried the young prophet in his own grave. The Bible does not tell us what happened to the wicked old prophet, but, barring repentance, we know he eventually ended in a fiery lake (Revelation 21:8).

People lie in personal relationships. Many people lie to those closest to them, despite the fact that Paul said, "Lie not one to another, seeing that you have put off the old man with his deeds; and have put on the new man, which is renewed in knowledge after the image of him that created him" (Colossians 3:9–10).

- 75% have lied to friends.
- 73% have lied to siblings.
- 69% have lied to spouses.
- 58% have lied to best friends.
- 49% have lied to neighbors.
- 32% have lied to doctors.
- 21% have lied to ministers.
- 20% have lied to lawyers.

People lie to themselves. The saddest of all lies is to lie to ourselves. The Bible speaks in several places of deceiving ourselves.

- We deceive ourselves if we hear the Word and do not do it (James 1:22).
- We deceive ourselves if we are religious but have unbridled tongues (James 1:26).
- To say we have no sin is to deceive ourselves (1 John 1:8).

WHY DO PEOPLE LIE?

Lies are self-serving. There are three broad categories as to why people lie: to gain favor from others by making others feel better about themselves, to boast and make ourselves look better, and to protect ourselves.

Some lie out of habit. Everybody knew the Cretans were always liars (Titus 1:12). Some lies are so common that a person may not even think twice before speaking them. "We unconsciously lie to people without thinking very much about it or even categorizing it as a lie," says Feldman.[13] Any of these sound familiar?

- "You look so good. You haven't changed in twenty years."
- "I can't make it in today. I'm really sick."
- "I lost that file when my computer crashed."
- "I tried you several times but the line was busy."
- "The check is in the mail."
- "I had a nice time tonight, too. I'll call you."

Chronic lying can signal a psychiatric or social disorder. If you find yourself lying for no reason or to cover up behavior that you know is harmful, consider seeking professional help.[14] Spiritually, becoming hard-hearted to any sin is a dangerous condition (cf. Hebrews 3:8–15; 4:7).

Some lie to be polite. People seem to think that lying is permissible under two conditions: (1) It does not harm anyone (an impossibility), and (2) it helps to promote a "good" cause (usually someone's personal agenda, career, or financial situation). Millions believe that white lies are harmless and confess they have told hundreds of them without any ill effects. Most people expect a certain amount of untruth. Aldous Huxley quipped, "You shall know the truth and the truth shall make you mad."[15] Have we used these insincerely?

- "No, that doesn't make you look fat."
- "That was a good sermon, preacher. I enjoyed it."
- "It's so good to see you."
- "I'll be there Sunday, for sure."
- "What a beautiful baby!"
- "I'm praying for you."

Some lie for convenience or out of laziness. O. C. Lambert writes of Catholic teachings that permit lies of convenience:

> So that a false statement knowingly made to one who has not a right to the truth will not be a lie . . . A Catholic maid may say "my mistress is not in" when in reality she is at home, but does not wish to see her caller . . . A Catholic may say to a beggar, "I wish I had it" when he has a pocketful of money.[16]

Others tell lies to avoid people or tasks they don't like:

- When a phone call comes at an inconvenient time, they say, "Tell them I'm not home."
- When the boss wants them to stay over on a project, they say, "I can't; I have a dentist appointment," when they really just want to go home.

Some lie to make themselves look better to others. The lies that Ananias and Sapphira told fall into this category (Acts 5:1–11). Oliver Herford said, "There are more fish taken out of a stream than ever were in it." A University of Massachusetts study found that most people lie during everyday conversations "to make themselves seem competent and appealing." In the study, which tested 121 pairs of people, 60 percent of the participants lied at least once during a ten-minute chat. This type of lying can be a sign of low self-esteem, problems at home, or depression.[17]

Some lie to protect themselves from embarrassment or disapproval. A little boy in Bible class was asked, "What is a lie?" He replied, "An abomination in the sight of God, and a very present help in time of trouble."[18]

A minister told his congregation, "Next week I plan to preach about the sin of lying. To help you understand my sermon, I want you all to read Mark 17." The following Sunday, before his sermon, the minister asked, "How many of you read Mark 17?" Hands went up all around the auditorium. He smiled and said, "Mark has only 16 chapters. I will now proceed with my sermon on lying." Cain lied to God when God asked where his brother Abel was. He said, "I know not" (Genesis 4:9) because he was trying to avoid the consequences of murdering his brother in a fit of rage.

Some lie to protect themselves from conflict or danger (Genesis 16:11–20). The most common reason that people lie is to avoid confrontation. Peter lied so he would not be arrested like Jesus (Matthew 26:57–75). Getting into hot water is undesirable, but lying to avoid it is a "band-aid" solution. When the truth comes out, the confrontation is guaranteed to be more unpleasant than it would have been without the lie. A lie compounds the problem; it doesn't solve it.[19]

Adults often deceive for exactly the same reasons as children: "to save their own skins or to get something they can't get by other means."[20] There are few negative remarks recorded in the Bible about Abraham, but on two occasions he lied about Sarah being his wife. He called her his sister to Pharaoh (Genesis 12:13) and later to Abimelech (Genesis 20:2). These lies were told to save his life, but they resulted in the near loss of Sarah's purity, and in plagues on Pharaoh's house (Genesis 12).

A man suing over an automobile and horse buggy accident was on the stand. The defendant's counsel took over. "Did you, or did you not," he asked the plaintiff, "at the time of the accident, when asked if you were hurt, reply that you weren't?"

"Well," said the plaintiff, "it was like this. I was going along the road with my old horse and wagon, and along comes this motorist and knocks us into the ditch. You never saw such a mess in all your life. There I was flat on my back with my legs in the air. There was my horse on his back, with his legs in the air. And there was my wagon with its wheels in the air. There was my dog, all cut up and whimpering. This motorist stops his car, gets out, and looks at us. He sees my horse with a broken leg. He goes back to his car, gets his pistol, and shoots him. He hears my dog whimpering, looks at him, and shoots him. Then he comes up to me and says, 'Now, how about you? Are you hurt?'"[21]

A child learns to lie in order to avoid punishment. He may have learned that lesson from his father who lied to the policeman about how fast he was going and then boasted about his cleverness in avoiding a fine.

Some lie to protect someone or to spare another's feelings. About 25 percent of lies fall into this category. While men and women lied the same amount according to one study, their motivations were different. Women fibbed to make the listener feel good; men did so to make themselves look better.[22] Rahab lied to protect the spies (Joshua 2:4–5), but should have told the truth and let God save the spies in another way.

Some lie to cover their shame. Perhaps this is why Potiphar's wife lied to her husband. She tried to entice Joseph, but he refused (Genesis 39).

Some lie in order to get money (2 Kings 5:22). *Fortune* magazine published a piece titled "The Art of Lying: Can It Be a Good Thing?" in which they said, "To win at business, you need to practice gaming ethics, which allows for tactics such as bluffing and artful negotiating that would be considered dishonest anywhere else."[23] Notice that when it is considered necessary for success, it is no longer called lying, but "gaming ethics," "bluffing," and "artful negotiating." God said it would be better to be a poor man than a liar (Proverbs 19:22).

Sometimes silence can be a lie. An item got by a clerk at a grocery store. A child was about to tell, but her mom whispered, "No, we get that one free." By contrast, consider a family who went to Six Flags Amusement Park. The two adults and three children were on their way out of the park when they noticed a sign they had not seen earlier. It said that the cut-off age for a discounted child's ticket was age ten. One of their children was eleven but had gotten a child's ticket. Since the ticket booth was closed, they mailed back the difference in the ticket prices when they got home. No Bible class on honesty could have made a better impression on that eleven-year-old.

Some lie to get an advantage over another (Genesis 27:18–25) or to persuade another to do something they want done (1 Kings 13:11–19). Many lie to gain position, power, and prestige. Others lie to win favor. Some lie to protect a friend, thinking themselves to be true friends by so doing. Often, the politician elected is the one who is the best liar.

Speaking of politicians, a joke illustrates the stereotype. A busload of politicians was driving down a country road, when the bus ran off the road and crashed into a tree in an old farmer's field. The old farmer, seeing what happened, went over to investigate. He proceeded to dig a hole and bury the politicians. A few days later the local sheriff came out, saw the crashed bus, and asked the farmer where all the politicians had gone. The old farmer said he had buried them. The sheriff then asked the old farmer, "Were they all dead?" The old farmer replied, "Well, some of them said they weren't, but you know how them politicians lie."

WHAT ARE THE CONSEQUENCES OF TELLING LIES?

Physical Consequences. Lying is abnormal and causes chaotic confusion in the nervous system of the body. The nervous system suffers a shock with every lie told (cf. 1 Corinthians 6:19–20). Lies damage self-image and cause inner conflicts—like dissonance—that drastically change the way one views and acts upon the world and other people.[24] A witness in court who tells a lie and covers it up with another is subjecting himself to terrible punishment. He becomes extremely nervous, which a lie detector may bring to light. On the other hand, one who tells the truth enjoys a calm, relaxed frame of mind, and his nerves experience no such disturbance. The remarkable self-control and calmness of Jesus under the stress of trial, accusation, and cross-examination indicate that He was telling the truth (e.g., Matthew 27:14).

Social Consequences. Solomon said that an ungodly man had words in his mouth as a "burning fire" (Proverbs 16:27). That fire soon gets out of his mouth and sets on fire his whole life (James 3:6). The consequence of fire is destruction of property; the consequence of a lie is destruction of persons. Lies cause war, break up homes, corrupt politics, interrupt or destroy Christian fellowship, and subject innocent people to punishment for crimes committed by others. Who could count the times that lies have caused the innocent to go to prison or even be executed? (e.g., 1 Kings 21:9–14). How often have we read of someone serving a ten- or twenty-year sentence before the lie that caused it was brought to light? The liar is a coward who does not have the courage to tell the truth and face the consequences. The wicked man's targets may lose their influence or their jobs. Truly, death resides in the power of a lying tongue (Proverbs 18:21). A lying tongue caused the death of the prophet of Judah (1 Kings 13:18–24).

A second social consequence of lies is the separating of friends (Proverbs 16:27–30; 17:4; 19:28). Separating friends can be done in several ways. One can dig up evil on someone to get even. One can lie about someone just to hurt him. One can slander, gossip, and backbite a competitor to win a prize or position. It is no wonder the psalmist said, "I hate and abhor lying: but thy law do I love" (119:163).

Spiritual Consequences. A liar forfeits fellowship with God (Isaiah 59:1–2; Revelation 21:27).

WHAT HAPPENS TO LIARS?

Caroline Keating, a Colgate University psychology professor, spent eighteen years studying liars. She reports that for those honest folks among us there is solace. Most liars and cheaters do get their comeuppance. Keating maintains, "Eventually deception is a dead end." She says, "People begin to believe their own manipulations and deceptions. And that can lead them to have very poor judgments."[25] The Bible says, "The lip of truth shall be established for ever: but a lying tongue is but for a moment" (Proverbs 12:19).

Both the Old and New Testaments clearly show God's severe hatred of untruths. The Bible says that liars will:

- **Be caught.** The wise man said, "A false witness shall not be unpunished, and he that speaketh lies shall not escape" (Proverbs 19:5).
- **Be stopped** (Psalm 63:11).
- **Be silenced** (Psalm 31:18).
- **Be cut off from the fellowship of the righteous** (Psalm 101:5).
- **Perish** (Proverbs 12:19; 19:9).
- **End in the lake of fire** (Revelation 21:8, 27). The result of believing a lie in religion is damnation (2 Thessalonians 2:12). So, "Be not deceived; God is not mocked: for whatsoever a man soweth, that shall he also reap" (Galatians 6:7).

One may work with his hands and worship with his heart, yet allow a loose tongue to close the doors of heaven.

Questions to Consider and Discuss

1. Which statement grabs you? Comment on it:
   a. "I said in my haste, All men are liars" (Psalm 116:11).
   b. Lying is like alcoholism. You are always recovering.
   c. If you tell the truth, you don't have to remember anything.
   d. Religious frauds are the worst liars.
   e. Eighty-six percent of teens lie to parents.
   f. Women lie to make the listener feel good; men lie to make themselves look better.
   g. "Repetition does not transform a lie into a truth" (Franklin Roosevelt).
   h. "The great masses of the people . . . will more easily fall victims to a big lie than to a small one" (Adolph Hitler).
   i. In a small town, everybody hears everything that happens and a whole lot that didn't.
   j. An honest man wants you to check him, and others you'd better.

2. Were you surprised to learn that, "Most people lie to others once or twice a day and deceive about 30 people per week," and, "In a single day, most of us lie . . . a minimum of 25 times"? Do you think this fits your personal situation? Why or why not?

3. Does your superior at work encourage honesty, or deception? In what ways?

4. Have you found it to be so that "men lie more than women and young men lie more than older men"?

5. What are some practical ways to teach our children and grandchildren always to be honest?

6. Which types of lies found on pages 26–27 do you find hardest to avoid?

7. Do you think there is such a thing as a "little white lie"?

8. Why do you think the old prophet lied to the young prophet? (1 Kings 13).

9. Do you agree that "stealing by telling a lie is just as wrong as stealing with a gun"?

10. How do you think that schools should handle cheating on tests and assignments? How do you think the IRS should handle lying on tax reports?

11. Did God condone Rahab's lie? (Joshua 2).

12. Do you think most business people believe, "To win at business, you need to practice gaming ethics, which allows for tactics such as bluffing and artful negotiating that would be considered dishonest anywhere else"?

CHAPTER FOUR

HANDS THAT SHED INNOCENT BLOOD (1)

W e live in a violent world. Every day newscasters spend most of their time reporting on war, murder, rape, assault, robbery, and other violent crimes. Jesus said that Satan "was a murderer from the beginning" (John 8:44). It surely did not take him long to have success in tempting man to shed blood. Little did Eve realize, as she submitted to the serpent's lies, that her firstborn son would become a murderer. She could not have foreseen the heart-rending sorrow that she would have as she placed a murdered son into the earth. Since then, rivers of blood have flowed on God's earth.

Who could count all the murders individuals have committed out of malice, spite, envy, and greed? The sad truth is, statistically speaking, living in one of America's major cities puts us in greater danger of being killed than the soldiers who fought in the Persian Gulf and Iraq Wars. Between 1980 and 2000, there were 352,000 murders—or non-negligent manslaughters.[1] In just one of those years, more than 21,900 murders occurred for which arrests were made, and 2,000 murders occurred where no arrests were made. Also, 147 law enforcement officers were killed in the line of duty, and 46,000 deaths occurred on the highways. Almost half of these (49.2 percent) were the result of driving under the influence of alcohol. Nearly 23,000 people were murdered with the deadly weapon of a drunk driver.

Who could measure the blood shed in war since Eden? Just in the twentieth century 37 million people have died in wars.[2] It has been calculated that in the last 3,500 years, there have only been 230 years of peace throughout the civilized world.

Who could measure the blood shed in atrocities, persecutions, repressions, rebellions, and holocausts? In the last century, 170 million people were murdered by their own governments or an enemy government.[3]

AN OVERVIEW OF MURDER FROM A BIBLICAL PERSPECTIVE: MURDER IN THE OLD TESTAMENT

The word *murder* (in various forms) is found thirty-seven times in the Bible.[4] *Kill* occurs 206 times. Jesus said, "Thou shalt do no murder" (Matthew 19:18), echoing what His Father had given as law to Moses and Israel (Exodus 20:13). When God selected ten commandments to be the foundation of all human responsibility, He included these four weighty words among them: "Thou shalt not kill."

The Bible is filled with murder. Its stories practically drip blood. The history of mankind is a history of bloodshed. Murder was the first recorded sin outside of the Garden of Eden, as the world's first baby grew up to murder his own brother in a fit of rage (Genesis 4:8). The first person who ever died on this planet was murdered. The first funeral on earth was not for an old person, but for a young man.

The world turned violent again in the days of Noah (Genesis 6:11). It was so dangerous in Abraham's time that he feared that he would be killed so another could take his wife (Genesis 12:12), which prompted him to lie. Later Isaac told the same lie for the same reason (Genesis 26:7). Esau was angry enough to murder his twin brother (Genesis 27:41), but he was denied the opportunity when Jacob fled to a far land. Joseph's brothers were jealous enough to premeditate murder against him, before being talked out of it by Reuben (Genesis 37:20–21). The Egyptians murdered the male babies of the Israelites in bondage (Exodus 1:22). Moses killed an Egyptian who was killing[5] a Hebrew (Exodus 2:11–12).

The list continues; the Philistines plotted to murder Samson (Judges 16:2). Samuel feared that Saul would kill him (1 Samuel 16:2). Saul tried to get his son and his servants to kill David (1 Samuel 19:1), and he later attempted to murder David with a javelin (1 Samuel 18:10–11; cf. Psalm 59:1). David orchestrated the murder of Uriah the Hittite (2 Samuel 11:15; 12:9). Absalom murdered his brother Amnon for raping his sister (2 Samuel 13:28–29). Solomon tried to kill Jeroboam (1 Kings 11:40). Jezebel had Naboth murdered so Ahab could have his vineyard (1 Kings 21:19).

Nameless people perpetrated murder against the helpless—widows, fatherless, poor, needy, and strangers (Psalm 10:8; 94:6; Job 24:14). Israel killed the prophets who were sent to them (Matthew 23:31; Luke 11:47). Even priests were accused of murder (Hosea 6:9).

MURDER IN THE NEW TESTAMENT

In the New Testament the story of bloodshed continues without a pause. Its chief character, Jesus, was the victim of a successful murder plot (Matthew 26:4; Acts 7:52). A murderer named Barabbas played a minor role in that great tragedy, too (Luke 23:18–25; Acts 3:14–19). Earlier, Herodias had Jesus' cousin John the Baptist killed because she did not like John's preaching (Matthew 14; Mark 6:19). Saul of Tarsus consented to the murder of Stephen (Acts 7:58–60), and likely murdered others (cf. 1 Timothy 1:13–15). Paul himself was the target of a murder plot (Acts 9:23–24); and he was later falsely thought to be a murderer (Acts 28:4). Herod Agrippa I "killed James the brother of John with the sword" (Acts 12:2).

Murder is one of the sins of the Gentiles (Romans 1:29), and it is one reason that God gave society laws (1 Timothy 1:9). Murder is a work of the flesh (Galatians 5:21). Jesus said that His kingdom was to be different from the way the world had been before. He said, "My kingdom is not of this world: if my kingdom were of this world, then would my servants fight" (John 18:36).

WHY IS MURDER WRONG?

Murder is wrong because life is sacred. God explained to Noah and his family as they left the ark, that for the first time man would be allowed to kill animals and eat them for food. Then He said, "Whoso sheddeth man's blood, by man shall his blood be shed: for in the image of God made he man" (Genesis 9:6). Since man is made in the image of God, then the taking of a man's life is the destruction of the most precious and the most holy thing in the world.

Murder is wrong because it steals God's sovereign right to control the world (Hebrews 9:27). Since God alone is judge, God alone should determine the court appointment.

WHY DO PEOPLE MURDER?

The Bible shows that people committed murder for the following reasons:

- To take another's wife (Genesis 12:12; 26:7; 2 Samuel 11).
- To take another's property (1 Kings 21:19; John 10:10).
- To take revenge on someone who had cheated them (Genesis 27:32–41).
- To secure a throne (2 Kings 15:25).
- To render a paid-for service (Deuteronomy 27:25; Ezekiel 22:12). In recent years, a woman was convicted of hiring a hit man to murder the mother of her daughter's rival for a cheerleading position at school. She hoped the woman's daughter would be too upset to compete.
- To satisfy anger (Numbers 22:29; Matthew 5:21–22). Cain slew Abel because his works were evil and his brother's righteous (1 John 3:12).
- To satisfy hatred (John 5:18).

HOW DO WE AVOID BECOMING MURDERERS?

Most of us probably feel confident that we will never become murderers, but many who felt the same way are now behind bars. However, avoiding murder involves more than just refraining from assaulting someone. Consider what God says before you dismiss this chapter as applying only to others.

Guard the heart against hatred. We do not have to physically end a life to harbor in the heart attitudes that foster all of the killings that go on in the world (1 John 3:11–15). Just as God considers lust to be the prelude to adultery (Matthew 5:28), so He considers hate to be the precursor to murder. John wrote, "Whosoever hateth his brother is a murderer: and ye know that no murderer hath eternal life abiding in him" (1 John 3:15). If one is going to avoid adultery, he must avoid lust in the heart. If one is to avoid murder or lesser injuries to another, he must keep hate from his heart.

The Lord said that if we are angry and hateful to anyone, He classifies us with murderers. Society is driven by vendettas. One bumper sticker said, "Go ahead and hit me. My daughter's a lawyer." Another old story about a woman who was bitten by a dog makes this point. When she went to the doctor, the doctor told her the dog had rabies, and that she would have to begin treatments immediately. However, she took out a pen and paper and began making a long list. "Madam," the doctor said, "we have a treatment for you. There's no need to make out a will." She replied, "Oh, this is not a will. It's a list of all the people I intend to bite!"

So how do we deal with grudges and hateful feelings? Since murder originates in the heart (Proverbs 23:7; Matthew 15:19; Mark 7:21), we must put our first line of defense at that position. Like the Pharisees, we might rather deal with externals than internals. We might say, "Well, I've never shot or stabbed my enemy. I have never put cyanide in her food or clubbed him from behind with a brass candlestick." But the Lord looks at our thoughts and feelings, too. He looks at the roots, not just at the fruits. He is not content to trim off the poison oak in our lives close to the ground; He wants to uproot the whole weed. He knows that long before we would club anyone over the head, we begin to wish them evil in our thoughts.

One man wrote,

> This morning I woke up. I went into the bathroom to brush my teeth and an amazing thing happened. I took the tube of toothpaste, squeezed it, and do you know what came out? Toothpaste. I kid you not. It wasn't mashed potatoes. It wasn't Jello. It wasn't scented topical muscle rub. Just white, minty toothpaste. God knows that when I put Him first in my life, the first thing that will come out of my life when I am put under pressure will be His love. When my life has been filled with the love, peace, longsuffering, patience, and kindness of God, then when I am squeezed by people, circumstances, challenges, troubles, and problems, the Lord knows that out of my life and out of your life will come expressions of His love and His grace.

What we put in our minds, comes out in our deeds (cf. Philippians 4:8).

Control anger (Proverbs 14:17; 19:11; Ecclesiastes 7:9). We live in an angry world. Road rage, drive-by shootings, and angry public outbursts are the order of the day. If we are forced to wait in a line when we weren't expecting to, we can grow fangs just standing there. What is this? What's with this store? What's with these people? Why can't they get out their checkbooks before the total is rung up? Why are they moving so slow?

What drives most people's anger?

- Hurt—injury.

- Hurry—frustration.

A typical concert piano has more than 240 strings that, when tuned and tightened, create a pull of forty-thousand pounds on the frame. Without the tension, there would be no beautiful music. Yet, too much pressure can crack the piano and destroy its sound. The piano models a good strategy for stress. Balance in work, exercise, diet, recreation, worship, and relationships keeps us in harmony. Over-commitments knock us out of tune and rob the music from our lives.[6]

How do I deal with restless, impatient anger? We need to think before we act. We could pay a counselor a good amount of money, but we'll never find any advice better than: "Wherefore, my beloved brethren, let every man be swift to hear, slow to speak, slow to wrath" (James 1:19). Thomas Jefferson said that when he was angry, he forced himself to count to ten. And when he was really angry, he would count to a hundred. There are times when we probably should count and count until we run out of numbers, lest we end up being sorry (cf. Proverbs 13:16).

A wise man pulls the cork out of the bottle of his frustrations and lets the anger drain out in God's presence. He brings the whole knotted, tangled, twisted-up mess of it to his heavenly Father. We can take it to the Lord in prayer. If Cain had taken a walk in the orchard or sat by a stream for an hour instead of calling his brother into the field, how different his life would have been. Instead of being a marked man and an outcast for the rest of his life, he could have come home to a family each night.

Anger is a normal human emotion. The word *anger* (in various forms) is found 269 times in the Bible. Even Jesus was angry on one occasion, perhaps more (Mark 3:5). God is angry "every day" (Psalm 7:11), but "his anger endureth but for a moment" (Psalm 30:5), at least in the case of penitents. We must control our anger lest it lead us to sin. Paul wrote, "Be ye angry, and sin not: let not the sun go down upon your wrath" (Ephesians 4:26).

According to Jesus, murder begins with anger.

> Ye have heard that it was said by them of old time, Thou shalt not kill; and whosoever shall kill shall be in danger of the judgment: But I say unto you, That whosoever is angry with his brother without a cause shall be in danger of the judgment: and whosoever shall say to his brother, Raca, shall be in danger of the council: but whosoever shall say, Thou fool, shall be in danger of hell fire

(Matthew 5:21–22).

Here murder is tracked to its lair, and the signpost is marked "anger."

The King declares that if anger is in the life of one of His subjects, this subject is in danger of judgment. Under the kingship of Jesus, if the possibility of murder lurks within the heart of man, it is counted as murder. We say, "If looks could kill . . ." but in a sense, they can. Anger and hatred are murderous things; they distort our eyes and our countenances so that our very faces reflect death.

Unresolved anger draws Satan into our lives and homes like raw meat draws a shark. If we let anger simmer overnight, we give the enemy of our soul a toehold in our lives (Ephesians 4:27). Have you seen rock climbers scale an almost vertical surface just by finding a place to set one toe or grab hold with two fingers? By harboring anger, we are giving Satan a place in our soul, and from that place he will be able to direct his destructive activities. Even overnight, he can take the opportunity to plant the terrible seeds of murder in an unguarded heart.

Think of Cain. God tried to reason with Cain. He tried to reassure and comfort this disappointed, angry man. And finally God gave him a serious warning. But Cain had nurtured the anger and bitterness in his heart for so long that even God standing in the pathway was not going to stop him. He walked right around God to kill his brother.

Learn to use a soft answer (Proverbs 15:1). In the *Sermon on the Mount*, we learn that murder proceeds from hatred to anger to words. Killing really begins with speaking ("raca," "fool," Matthew 5:22). Words do hurt. In a sense, words can kill (Proverbs 18:21; cf. 17:22). Words can devastate a person's life. They can wipe a smile off a face. They can take the sparkle out of an eye. They can steal hope out of a heart. They can sour a friendship and sever a fellowship. They can cast a shadow over a beautiful day. They can quench those little sparks of fun and joy and laughter and tenderness that make life worth living. James wrote, "But the tongue can no man tame; it is an unruly evil, full of deadly poison" (James 3:8).

Remove opportunities. Solomon said, "Make no friendship with an angry man; and with a furious man thou shalt not go" (Proverbs 22:24). Jesus told Peter, "Put up again thy sword into his place: for all they that take the sword shall perish with the sword" (Matthew 26:52). When Paul and Barnabas had a "sharp contention" between them, they parted ways for a time (Acts 15:39). If one has violent feelings toward someone, then he should take steps to avoid this person; if he must be in the proximity, remove anything that might be used to injure.

WHAT IS THE PENALTY FOR MURDER?

Just after Noah and his family stepped off the plank that led down from the ark, God said, "Whoso sheddeth man's blood, by man shall his blood be shed" (Genesis 9:6; cf. Leviticus 17:11). Before this historical moment, murder was already forbidden, of course. God had placed a mark on Cain and warned that whoever killed him would face sevenfold vengeance (Genesis 4:11–15).

Punishment was finally codified in Moses' Law. A murderer was put to death under Moses' Law, by the avenger of blood (Numbers 35:16–21; Leviticus 24:17), provided there were at least two witnesses to testify against him (Numbers 35:30). Courts were forbidden to commute the sentence of a murderer for any amount of money (Numbers 35:31; Leviticus 24:21). In cases of manslaughter, arrangement was made for one to flee to a city of refuge (Numbers 35:11, 15; Deuteronomy 19:4–10). God says the murderer should be punished because he took that which God said is sacred— human life.

The popular idea today is completely opposite. After one has been killed, the murderer is brought to trial, and then the murderer's life is considered to be precious. God says that when a murderer kills a man, he is to forfeit his own life. In the New Testament, Jude said, "Woe unto them! for they have gone in the way of Cain" (Jude 11). Murderers are among those excluded from heaven (Revelation 22:15) and sent to the lake of fire (Revelation 21:8). Of course, murder, like other sins, can be forgiven. Those who murdered Jesus were forgiven (Acts 2:22–41).

Questions to Consider and Discuss:

1. What do you think would help curb the violence in our society?

2. Which statement would you like to discuss further?

   a. Living in one of America's major cities puts us in greater danger of being killed than the soldiers who fought in the Persian Gulf and Iraq Wars.

   b. If Cain had taken a walk in the orchard or sat by a stream for an hour instead of calling his brother into the field, how different his life would have been.

   c. "My kingdom is not of this world: if my kingdom were of this world, then would my servants fight" (John 18:36). (Relate it to the Crusades, abortion clinic bombings, and the "Holy Wars" of Islam.)

   d. "Whosoever hateth his brother is a murderer: and ye know that no murderer hath eternal life abiding in him" (1 John 3:15). Is it possible to be in the church services each Sunday and yet miss heaven as a "murderer"?

   e. Unresolved anger draws Satan into our lives and homes like raw meat draws a shark.

   f. "Make no friendship with an angry man; and with a furious man thou shalt not go" (Proverbs 22:24). Look at the angle of avoiding certain people and certain situations because they lead to violence.

3. Which Old Testament character are you most surprised to see give in to the temptation of violence and murder?

4. Why is murder wrong? Go beyond, "Because God said so."

5. What are some practical ways to get beyond hurts and resentments that might lead to violence?

6. What are some practical ways to overcome anger that could lead to violence? (cf. Ephesians 4:26; James 1:19).

HANDS THAT SHED INNOCENT BLOOD (2)

An analysis of the phrase
"Hands that shed innocent blood"

AND HANDS . . .

The word *hands* in the Bible is often used to stand for a person's deeds (cf. Psalm 7:3; 18:20, 24; 24:4; 26:6, 10; 73:13; 1 Timothy 2:8; James 4:8). This is a figure of speech called a *metonymy*. We use metonymies all the time. If a ranch foreman is asked, "How many hands do you have working for you?" he knows the person means, "How many workers do you have?" Solomon had in mind someone whose hands have been sullied with the blood of an innocent person. Isaiah wrote, "And when ye spread forth your hands, I will hide mine eyes from you: yea, when ye make many prayers, I will not hear: your hands are full of blood" (Isaiah 1:15; cf. 59:3–6; Psalm 125:3).

Compare that description with the hands of Jesus. They were placed on the heads of little children to bless them (Matthew 18:1–3; 19:13–14). They gave sight to the blind (Mark 8:23). At their touch, leprosy fled (Matthew 8:3) and the dead arose (Matthew 9:25). His hands fed the hungry multitude (Matthew 14:19), restored the severed ear of Malchus (Matthew 26:51), and freely sacrificed the precious blood that cancels all our sin (John 20:25–27).

THAT SHED . . .

The verb implies that one has actively injured another. He is not talking about accidents or helpful medical procedures. Still, shed would include abortion.

INNOCENT . . .

All murder is killing; but not all killing is murder.[1] Barclay points out that the Law of Moses distinguished at least four types of homicide.

First, there was justifiable homicide, or self-defense. If a thief was killed in the act of stealing, the one who smote him was not to be punished (Exodus 22:2–3; Acts 23:12–24).

Second, there was accidental homicide. Jewish law made special provision for what might be called non-deliberate killing—killing which happened by accident—such as the result of a blow or an attack which was not meant to kill. If two men were working together and one's axe head flew off the handle and killed his partner or one unintentionally caused a rock to fall which crushed his partner to death, no act of murder was involved (Numbers 35:22–28).

This person could flee to one of six cities of refuge and claim sanctuary until the facts of the case were known (Exodus 21:12–13; Numbers 35:6–34; Deuteronomy 4:41–43; 19:1–13; Joshua 20:1–9). The cities were so distributed that one would normally be no more than thirty miles from a city of refuge. Entrance into one of these cities did not offer limitless asylum, though. The person could not be handed over to the avenging next of kin of the dead man until the circumstances of the killing had been investigated. If it was found that the killing had been deliberate and premeditated, then the murderer had to be killed. God is against the act of murder and the one who commits it. If it was judged accidental, then the killer could live in the city of refuge and be free from the avenger of blood. If the killer ventured outside the city, the avenger might take his life (Numbers 35:9–28). When the high priest died and was replaced, the killer could return home and not be assaulted by the dead person's family.

Human life is of value because it is human life, whether one is of high station or from the lowest strata of society. Taking human life is never made legal by the privilege of power or plea of poverty. Achan, for instance, did not lose his life by the volition of his fellowmen. He was stoned to death by the will of God at the hands of men. No sanctuary was to be found on the face of the earth for a murderer. But if the killing could be proved accidental, if it came from a blow or a push or even a stab that was not meant to kill, if something had been thrown and had killed a man accidentally, then life could be spared. Note also, in passing, that even accidental killing was not looked upon as a light offense. The man who took life in this way was denied his liberty for an indefinite term. He would likely have to stay in the walls of the city of refuge for the rest of his life, unless the high priest was much older than he.

Third, there was **judicial homicide.** "Thou shalt not kill" does not forbid a policeman's or soldier's killing to protect others, nor a magistrate's putting offenders to death. These things tend to preserve life. Terrorists bomb buildings, hijack planes, and poison innocent people; civilian and military representatives of the United States are vulnerable to kidnapping and assassination in parts of the world; senseless and brutal murders take place in every city in our own nation.

Rehabilitation is not the relevant topic when dealing with murderers; the issue is justice. The Jews were forbidden to show pity to anyone who committed deliberate homicide (Deuteronomy 19:13). We make a mistake when we make no distinction between villain and victim and have as much compassion for the cold-blooded killer as for the innocent person whose life has been taken. Law is the foundation of society; therefore, for the sake of society, any breach of law or any defiance of it must be punished.

- If a crime has been committed which has caused loss or injury to someone, there must be restoration and restitution.
- It would be an intolerable situation if the criminal was allowed to profit by his crime. Concern for the criminal must not cause the victim to be entirely forgotten.
- Punishment is necessary as a deterrent.

It is necessary to demonstrate to anyone contemplating a crime that crime does not pay. Punishment is intended not only to punish the wrongdoer, but also to deter others from a similar course of action. It is this side of the matter which accounts for the element of publicity which often accompanies punishment. In Palestine, it was the custom to take a criminal to the place of execution by the longest possible route, so that as many as possible might see what happened to the man who broke the law. In modern times, newspapers, television, radio, and the Internet serve the same function. In some cases the publicity is the worst part of the punishment.

There must be a difference made between "innocent" blood and "guilty" blood. God does not hate all bloodshed. In fact, He commanded bloodshed in the case of capital punishment (Genesis 9:6; Exodus 21:12–14; 1 Kings 2:5–6, 28–34; Revelation 13:10). If "thou shalt not kill" (Exodus 20:13) and "hands that shed innocent blood" (Proverbs 6:17) were unqualified prohibitions, they would forbid anyone to carry out the penalty for their violation! (Deuteronomy 19:11–13). In the Hebrew the verb implies, as Driver puts it, "violent and unauthorized killing."[2]

Did this change in the New Testament? When Pilate asked Jesus, "Do you not know that I have power to release you, and power to crucify you?" Jesus did not say, "You don't have the right to the death penalty." He acknowledged that right, but denied that He was guilty and thus subject to it. Jesus admitted that Pilate had authority, and reminded Pilate of who gave him that authority (John 19:10–11).

About a quarter century later, Paul was on trial before Festus (Acts 25:11). He, too, acknowledged the death penalty, but claimed innocence. About four years before his trial before Festus (A.D. 56), Paul had written to the Roman Christians about the functions of civil government. Through him, God said one function of government included "bearing the sword" to "execute wrath" on evildoers: "For he is the minister of God to thee for good. But if thou do that which is evil, be afraid; for he beareth not the sword in vain: for he is the minister of God, a revenger to execute wrath upon him that doeth evil" (Romans 13:4).

Both testaments were written by the same God. He was not a vengeful God in the Old Testament, who somehow changed to a loving God in the New Testament (cf. Hebrews 13:8). In Exodus 32 God in effect commissioned the tribe of Levi to be a police force to deal with idolatry in the camp. They put to death about three thousand offenders that very day. It should also be noted that the Bible does not sanction police brutality, or execution for just any crime. There have been abuses of capital punishment (for instance, by the guillotine in France or by the gallows or the headsman's block in Britain).

Consider some excerpts from *The Ten Commandments for Today*[3] by William Barclay:

"Within the Jewish legal system it was never even suggested that this commandment forbade what may be called judicial killing. W. H. Bennett in the article on

Hebrew crimes and punishment in James Hastings' *Encyclopedia of Religion and Ethics* conveniently lists the Jewish crimes which were regarded as being liable to the death penalty, and the particular way in which in each case the death penalty was carried out, where that way was known. The capital crimes under ancient Jewish law were:

1. Murder (Exodus 21:12; Leviticus 24:17).

2. Child sacrifice (Leviticus 20:2; death by stoning).

3. Manslaughter (Numbers 35:9–28). The "avenger of blood" could kill the one who killed his near kinsman if the killer was outside the city of refuge.

4. Keeping an ox known to be dangerous, if the ox killed a man (Exodus 21:29).

5. Bearing false witness on a capital charge (Deuteronomy 19:18–21).

6. Kidnapping or stealing a man (Exodus 21:16; Deuteronomy 24:7).

7. Insult or injury to parents (Exodus 21:17; Leviticus 20:9; Deuteronomy 21:18–21; death by stoning).

8. Various forms of sexual immorality:
   a. Incest, which was defined as intercourse with mother, stepmother, half-sister, granddaughter, stepsister, aunt, uncle's wife, daughter-in-law, sister-in-law, stepdaughter, step-granddaughter, mother-in-law (death by burning).
   b. Unchastity before marriage, discovered after marriage (Deuteronomy 22:21–24; death by stoning).
   c. Adultery, bestiality, homosexuality, and unnatural vice (Leviticus 18:23; 20:10–16; Exodus 22:19; Ezekiel 16:38, 40; John 8:5).
   d. Fornication by a priest's daughter (Leviticus 21:9; death by burning).
   e. Fornication by a betrothed woman (Deuteronomy 22:22, death by stoning; Genesis 38:24, death by burning).

9. Various religious and ritual offenses:
   a. Witchcraft and magic (Exodus 22:18; Leviticus 20:6, 27; death by stoning)
   b. Idolatry (Exodus 22:20; Deuteronomy 13:6–11; death by stoning).
   c. Blasphemy (Leviticus 24:10–16; death by stoning).
   d. False claims to be a prophet (Deuteronomy 13:5, 10; death by stoning).

e. Intrusion of an alien into a sacred place or office (Numbers 1:51; 3:10; 18:7).

f. Sabbath-breaking (Exodus 31:14).

*Fourth, there was **premeditated murder** (Numbers 35:16–21).* This is planning ahead of time, lying in wait, taking the person off guard, and slaying him. It is also killing a person in the course of committing some other crime against him, such as trying to rob him. It includes all killings of malice and hatred. The bloodshed under consideration here is of those who did not deserve injury, punishment, or death. Saul was asked: "Wherefore then wilt thou sin against innocent blood, to slay David without a cause?" (1 Samuel 19:5). Take Manasseh for another example: "Manasseh . . . filled Jerusalem with innocent blood; which the LORD would not pardon" (2 Kings 24:3–4). The pagan mariners who found Jonah aboard were afraid to shed "innocent blood" (Jonah 1:14). Even hard-hearted Judas came to regret betraying "innocent blood" (Matthew 27:4).

BLOOD . . .

"Life is in the blood" is a key concept in the Bible (Leviticus 17:11, 14; Deuteronomy 12:23; Matthew 26:28; Acts 20:28; Romans 3:25; 5:9; Ephesians 1:7). The word *blood* is found 447 times in the Bible—101 times in the New Testament. God told Moses: "Whoso sheddeth man's blood, by man shall his blood be shed: for in the image of God made he man" (Genesis 9:6).[4]

The phrase *shed blood* is found fifteen times in Scripture—fourteen times in the Old Testament; once in the New Testament. Abigail met an angry David to prevent him from shedding her husband's blood (1 Samuel 25:26, 33). Because David had "shed blood abundantly" in war, God forbade him from building the house of worship (1 Chronicles 22:8; 28:3). Solomon warned his son not to get in the company of those who "made haste to shed blood" (Proverbs 1:16). One part of Paul's description of the universal sinfulness of man includes "feet that are swift to shed blood" (Romans 3:15).

Questions to Consider and Discuss:

1. Do you believe that removing God and the Bible from schools and society has contributed to the increase in violence and murder? What effect has teaching evolution to school children for the last one hundred years had on society?

2. What are the four types of homicide included in the Law of Moses?

3. Choose a statement to discuss further in class:
   a. All murder is killing; but not all killing is murder.
   b. We make a mistake when we make no distinction between villain and victim and have as much compassion for the cold-blooded killer as for the innocent person whose life has been taken.

4. Were you surprised at the number of offenses that brought the death penalty under Old Testament Law? Which ones surprised you the most?

5. Does the command, "Thou shalt not kill" forbid capital punishment? Does it forbid abortion?

6. Discuss the difference made between "innocent" blood and "guilty" blood.

7. Discuss the importance of the phrase, "Life is in the blood."

8. Role play: A class member has a friend who has killed someone in an automobile accident. Give practical advice on how to counsel the friend to overcome guilt and go on with life.

CHAPTER SIX

GOD'S VIEW OF ABORTION

During the darkest days of Israel's history, God's own nation turned to idolatry—and not just idolatry, but idolatry in its worst form. They actually sacrificed their own children in the worship of Molech (2 Kings 23:10; cf. Psalm 106:37–46). What was involved in worshipping Molech? Don't picture padded pews and a priest offering some "love thy neighbor" platitudes. Don't think of a collection basket passed around for everyone to put a few shekels in. Don't picture a quick service and off to the nearest restaurant. No, the worship of Molech was pagan to the core—and the worst kind of paganism.

According to Jewish tradition, the image of Molech was a hollow brass statue placed outside of Jerusalem. Josephus quotes Kimchi as describing the idol as being inside seven chapels. If a worshiper offered fine flour, he got to go into the first chapel. If he offered turtledoves or young pigeons, he made it to the second; if he gave a lamb, they opened to him the third room; if he sacrificed a ram, he made it to the fourth; if he gave a calf, he went as far as the fifth chapel; if he gave an ox, they opened to him the sixth chapel. But only those who offered a son made it to the seventh chapel.

The idol's body was said to look like a calf, and his hands were stretched out like a man who opened his arms to receive something. They kindled a fire inside the hollow statue to make the metal burning hot. Then the priests took the baby and "put it into the hands of Molech, and the babe gave up the ghost." It is little wonder that *Matthew Henry's Commentary on the Whole Bible* refers to Molech as the "god of unnatural cruelty" in contrast with other gods of "unnatural uncleanness" (Volume 3, Hendrickson Publishers).

Jeremiah wrote of this: "And they have built the high places of Tophet, which is in the valley of the son of Hinnom, to burn their sons and their daughters in the fire; which I commanded them not, neither came it into my heart" (Jeremiah 7:31). Why was it called "the places of *Tophet*" and "the valley of . . . Hinnom"? "Because they used to make a noise with drums (*tophim*), that the father might not hear the cry of his child and have pity upon him and return to him. Hinnom, because the babe wailed (*menahem*) and the noise of his wailing went up."[1]

In modern, civilized America, we are shocked that anyone could be so inhuman. But then we turn our attention to our own atrocities. Every twenty-one seconds an unborn child is murdered in our country. Oh, we don't call it "murder;" we don't even call it a "baby." We use terms like "terminate," "extract," "fetus," "tissue," and "abortion." Although the terms sound clean and scientific, the act is still murder. The abortion issue seems to have been in the newspapers and on newscasts practically every day for the past three decades. Showdowns occur in front of clinics, in the Capitol's streets, in the halls of Congress, in voting booths, and in the Supreme Court's chambers.

Abortion is a modern example of "hands that shed innocent blood" (Proverbs 6:17). It is the worst kind of murder—the slaughter of the innocent and helpless, the murder of little babies.

WHAT IS ABORTION?

Abortion is defined as "the expelling of the fetus from the uterus."[2] It can happen naturally—spontaneous abortion, as in a fall or accident—or it can be externally induced. In this lesson, we are discussing invading the womb and deliberately terminating the life of an unborn child.

WHAT IS THE HISTORY OF ABORTION?

History in a broad perspective. Americans tend to think of abortion as modern. It is not. Life was cheap in many ancient cultures. Unwanted or deformed infants were routinely exposed to the elements and left to die in Greek and Roman times. Abortion was practiced by many ancient pagans. It has been practiced by barbarians since early in the world's history—at least since the time of Abraham. Civilized nations have generally outlawed it.

- The Code of Hammurabi (eighteenth century B.C.), Mosaic Law (sixteenth century B.C.), Tiglath-pileser of Persia (twelfth century B.C.), the Greek physician, Hippocrates, Seneca (second century A.D.), Augustine (fourth century), Thomas Aquinas (thirteenth century), and John Calvin (sixteenth century) all took positions against abortion or intentionally causing the death of the unborn.
- "English common law exacted a punishment for taking life by abortion, as did early American law. In fact, before 1973, laws in nearly all fifty states opposed abortion."[3]

History in America. On January 22, 1973 nine black-robed men issued a death decree that lives in infamy. In the 1973 *Roe v. Wade*[4] decision, the Supreme Court ruled that women, in consultation with their physicians, have a constitutionally protected right to have an abortion in the early stages of pregnancy—that is, before viability—free from government interference. This U.S. Supreme Court decision eliminated any protection for an unborn child's life in favor of a mother's right to privacy.

- During the first three months of pregnancy the decision to abort rests solely with the woman and her doctor;
- During the second three months, the State can regulate the abortion procedure to protect maternal health;
- During the third three months, when the fetus is viable, the State can regulate or even prohibit abortion except when it is necessary for the mother's mental or physical health.[5]

Note that with a doctor's permission and use of the "mental or physical health" loophole (what mother's mental and physical health is not threatened during childbirth?), an abortion is legal throughout the entire forty weeks of pregnancy—up to the day of birth. It is true that the majority of abortions are performed in the first trimester, but many still occur in the second and third trimesters. The Alan Guttmacher Institute, which, according to their mission statement, favors the "freedom to terminate unwanted pregnancies," states that 12 percent occur after twelve weeks of pregnancy. That is more than 150,000 babies a year. It further indicates that some 13,700 of these abortions took place at twenty-one weeks or more.[6] Many babies delivered at this stage of development can survive.

In 1992, the Court upheld the right to abortion in *Planned Parenthood v. Casey.* However, the ruling significantly weakened the legal protections previously afforded women and physicians by giving states the right to enact restrictions that do not create an "undue burden" for women seeking abortion.

- Thirty-two states currently enforce parental consent or notification laws for minors seeking an abortion: AL, AR, AZ, DE, GA, IA, ID, IN, KS, KY, LA, MA, MD, MI, MN, MO, MS, NC, ND, NE, OH, PA, RI, SC, SD, TN, TX, UT, VA, WI, WV, and WY. The Supreme Court ruled that minors must have the alternative of seeking a court order authorizing the procedure.[7]
- Only 45 percent of minors who have abortions tell both parents; 61 percent undergo the procedure with at least one parent's knowledge. The great majority of these parents support their daughter's decision.[8]

In *Stenberg v. Carhart* (2000), the Court declared Nebraska's law criminalizing so-called partial birth abortion unconstitutional because it lacked an exception to protect the woman's health. The Court also found that the law imposed "an undue burden" (see 1992 *Planned Parenthood v. Casey*) on women because it was written so broadly as to ban not only dilation and extraction (D&X) procedures, but also dilation and evacuation (D&E) procedures.

In September 2000, the U.S. Food and Drug Administration approved the abortion drug mifepristone to be marketed in the United States as an alternative to surgical abortion.

- About 37,000 medical abortions were performed in the first half of 2001; these procedures involved the use of mifepristone or methotrexate.
- Approximately 600 providers offered medical abortion in the first half of 2001.
- In non-hospital facilities offering mifepristone for use in medical abortion in 2000, the average cost of a medical abortion was $490.[9]

Because of such court decisions, "they that work wickedness are set up" (Malachi 3:15). Regardless of what has been declared legal by human governments, God's Word trumps every court decision. Jesus said, "Ye are they which justify yourselves before men; but God knoweth your hearts: for that which is highly esteemed among men is abomination in the sight of God" (Luke 16:15). Peter would still say today, "We ought to obey God rather than men" (Acts 5:29).

Isaiah said, "Woe unto them that call evil good,[10] and good evil; that put darkness for light, and light for darkness; that put bitter for sweet, and sweet for bitter!" (Isaiah 5:20; cf. Matthew 15:3–6). God is "wearied" by men who say, "Every one that doeth evil is good in the sight of the LORD, and he delighteth in them; or, Where is the God of judgment?" (Malachi 2:17). A wiser man than any Supreme Court justice said, "He that justifieth the wicked, and he that condemneth the just, even they both are abomination to the LORD" (Proverbs 17:15). Paul warned, "This know also, that in the last days perilous times shall come. For men shall be . . . without natural affection" (2 Timothy 3:1–3).

HOW MANY ABORTIONS TAKE PLACE EACH YEAR?

Abortion is legal in fifty-four of the ninety-seven major countries of the world—these countries have 61 percent of the world's population. Have we stopped to consider how utterly horrific the abortion statistics are?

Consider the following:

- Worldwide, there are approximately 46 million abortions conducted each year; 1,370,000 abortions occur annually in the U.S.
- Worldwide, there are approximately 126,000 abortions conducted each day. In the U.S. there are approximately 3,753 abortions a day; 156 per hour, 2 per minute. Think of that! In our "Christian nation," a baby is murdered every thirty seconds around the clock, seven days a week, year in and year out!
- Each year in America, 2 out of every 100 women aged 15–44 have an abortion; 48 percent of them have had at least one previous abortion and 61 percent have had a previous birth.[11]
- In the U.S., 43 percent of women will have had at least one abortion by age 45.

America's policy is the most liberal in the western world. Except for biopsies, abortion is the most common surgical procedure performed in the U.S. One child in three dies by abortion in the U.S.[12] The most dangerous place for a child in America is inside the child's mother.

The mother's womb has become the baby's tomb. Jeremiah, in a state of depression, wished "that my mother might have been my grave, and her womb to be always great with me" (Jeremiah 20:17). This sad dream has become a reality for millions and millions of unloved children. The Bible condemns those who are without "natural affection"[13] (Romans 1:31; 2 Timothy 3:3). The National Vietnam Memorial in Washington D.C., is a shiny black wall that stretches 492 feet and lists the names of the 58,022 known Americans killed in that war. If such a wall listed the names of the children killed by abortion since 1973, the wall would be about sixty miles long! The casualties of our wars put together are fewer than the casualties from abortion in a single year.

HOW MUCH MONEY IS INVOLVED?

On average, an abortion costs $372 for a self-paying woman obtaining a surgical abortion at 10 weeks LMP (from her last menstrual period). It cost about $200 for the same abortion in 1983. Abortions performed at 16 weeks typically cost $774, while those at 20 weeks ran $1,179. Employing such estimates, the average abortionist with a caseload of a thousand first-trimester surgical abortions a year brings in a minimum of $372,000. If he does more, if he charges more, or if he does later abortions, that figure grows dramatically.

About $500 million changes hands for abortions in this country annually, and about one-third of abortuaries are tax exempt. The U.S. Congress has barred the use of federal Medicaid funds to pay for abortions, except when the woman's life would be endangered by a full-term pregnancy, or in cases of rape or incest.[14] Seventeen states[15] do use public funds to pay for abortions for some poor women. About 14 percent of all abortions in the United States are paid for with public funds—virtually all from the state.[16]

There were 2,380 abortionists in 1992, 2,042 in 1996, and 1,819 in 2000, according to the Alan Guttmacher Institute. The figure for 2000 represents a drop of 11 percent from the 1996 survey and a decrease of over 37 percent from the all-time high of 2,908 recorded in 1982. Some drop out because of "harassment" from abortion foes. Others get out of the business because they can no longer face the reality of what they are doing.[17] The same reality that drove NARAL founder Dr. Bernard Nathanson out of the abortion clinic and into the ranks of pro-lifers has gradually worn on abortionists and thinned their ranks.

Even the *New York Times* called abortion a "tough thing for gynecologists" and said the emotions it arouses are so strong that doctors "don't talk to each other about" it.[18] The *Washington Post* wrote that older doctors doing abortions were disillusioned because they got in thinking of abortion "as a breakthrough in women's health and a means to prevent the birth of babies with severe genetic defects" but later came to believe it had become used as "after-the-fact birth control."[19] The dearth of abortionists is one of the reasons behind the industry's push for mandatory abortion training in medical schools and efforts to recruit new "providers" who would use the abortion pill RU-486. As much as 43 percent of the decline in abortion between 1994 and 2000 can be attributed to the use of emergency contraception—morning after pill.[20]

God said, "Cursed be he that taketh reward to slay an innocent person" (Deuteronomy 27:25; cf. Psalm 15:5; Matthew 26:15), and "the innocent and righteous slay thou not: for I will not justify the wicked" (Exodus 23:7).

WHAT GOES ON IN AN ABORTION CLINIC?

What is the best way to learn about abortion? To actually witness an abortion or to work in a clinic would give first-hand insight. The second best way is to read verified eye-witness accounts from people who are current or former abortion providers. These quotes have been tracked down from a number of sources, from the research of pro-choice author Magda Denes to the *Washington Post* to other magazines.[21] One can verify the facts of fetal development in an encyclopedia or reference book.[22] Consider some quotes from those who work or have worked in abortion clinics:[23]

- "I was trained by a professional marketing director in how to sell abortions over the telephone. He took every one of our receptionists, nurses, and anyone else who would deal with people over the phone through an extensive training period. The object was, when the girl called, to hook the sale so that she wouldn't get an abortion somewhere else, or adopt out her baby, or change her mind. We were doing it for the money" (Nina Whitten, chief secretary at a Dallas abortion clinic).

- "In my facilities, I always gave option counseling. Of course you make the abortion the most appealing. I told them about adoption and about foster care and about [when there was welfare] assistance. The typical way it would go is, 'Well, you know you can place your baby out for adoption.' But then, in the second breath you would say, 'That's an option available to you, but you also have to realize that there's going to be a baby of yours out here somewhere in the world you will never see again. At least with abortion you know what's happening. You can go on with your life . . . ' The longer I was in it, the less I cared, so I didn't really care what my conscience said. My conscience was totally numb anyway. But what it did do was public relations-wise. You were able, when a reporter or TV crew came, to pull out a packet of information for the patients to read and [say] they received it. So what can anybody say? Publicly it looked good—in reality it was another tool that was used to force a woman into abortion. It's typical—I would give them an option and then shoot it down. The only option you didn't shoot down, obviously, was abortion" (former abortionist Eric Harrah, quoted by Dr. Jack Wilke and Brad Mattes).

- "They are never allowed to look at the ultrasound because we knew that if they so much as heard the heart beat, they wouldn't want to have an abortion" (Dr. Randall "Pro-Choice 1990: Skeletons in the Closet" by David Kuperlain and Mark Masters in October *New Dimensions* magazine).

- "We tried to avoid the women seeing them [the fetuses]. They always wanted to know the sex, but we lied and said it was too early to tell. It's better for the women to think of the fetus as an 'it'" (Abortion clinic worker Norma Eidelman, quoted in *Rachel Weeping*, page 34).[24]

- "Sometimes we lied. A girl might ask what her baby was like at a certain point in the pregnancy: Was it a baby yet? Even as early as 12 weeks a baby is totally formed, he has fingerprints, turns his head, fans his toes, feels pain. But we would say 'It's not a baby yet. It's just tissue, like a clot'" (Kathy Sparks, told in "The Conversion of Kathy Sparks" by Gloria Williamson, *Christian Herald*, January 1986, p. 28).

- "I have seen hundreds of patients in my office who have had abortions and were just lied to by the abortion counselor. Namely 'This is less painful than having a tooth removed. It is not a baby.' Afterwards, the woman sees *Life* magazine and breaks down and goes into a major depression" (Psychologist Vincent Rue, quoted in "Abortion Inc.," David Kupelian and Jo Ann Gasper, *New Dimensions*, October 1991, page 16).

- "From May to November 1988, I worked for an abortionist. He specializes in third trimester killings. I witnessed evidence of the brutal, cold-blooded murder of over 600 viable, healthy babies at seven, eight, and nine months' gestation. A very, very few of these babies, less than 2 percent, were handicapped . . . I thought I was pro-choice and I was glad to be working in an abortion clinic. I thought I was helping provide a noble service to women in crisis. . . . I was instructed to falsify the age of the babies in medical records. I was required to lie to the mothers over the phone, as they scheduled their appointments, and to tell them that they were not 'too far along.' Then I had to note, in the records that Dr. [name withheld] needle had successfully pierced the walls of the baby's heart, injecting the poison that brought death . . . One day, Dr. [name withheld] came up the stairs from the basement, where the mothers were in labor. He was carrying a large cardboard box, and ducked into the employee's only area of the office so that he wouldn't have to walk through the waiting room. He passed behind my desk as I sat working on the computer, and he turned the corner to go around a short hall. He called out for me to come and help him. The box was so big and heavy in his arms that he couldn't get the key into the lock. So I unlocked the door for him, and, pushing the door open, I saw very clearly the gleaming metal of the crematorium—a full sized crematorium, just like the ones used in funeral homes. I went back to my computer. I could hear Dr. [name withheld] firing up the gas oven. A few minutes later I could smell burning human flesh. Mine was the agony of a participant, however reluctant, in the act of prenatal infanticide" (Luhra Tivis, now a member of Operation Rescue, on her experience in the abortion business, *Celebrate Life,* September/October 1994, "Where is the Real Violence?").

• "You're going from dealing with people to dealing with what most people here at the Center consider a real hurdle, to do sterile room, because you have to deal with the actual abortion tissue. And for some people, that's really hard. They can be abstractly in favor of abortion rights, but they sure don't want to see what an eighteen-week abortion looks like."

• "It's just—I mean it looks like a baby. It looks like a baby. And especially if you get one that comes out, that's not piecemeal. And you know, I saw this one, and it had its fingers in its mouth . . . it makes me really sad that that had to happen, you know, but it doesn't change my mind. It's just hard. And it makes me just sort of stop and feel sad about it, the whole necessity of it. And also . . . it's very warm when it comes into the sterile room because it's been in the mother's stomach. It feels like flesh, you know . . ."

- "It's going to be weird now because you're going to see the sono. You're going to see the heart beating—little hearts, you know—and then, all of a sudden, you're going to put his cardiac medicine in it to make it stop—to kill it. So you're going to see the exact moment when you kill the fetus. I won't kill it, the doctor will kill it . . . [if] the fetuses do feel something, why not kill it, you know, fast, [rather] than rip its leg off?"

Norma McCorvey, the "Jane Roe" of the *Roe vs. Wade* 1973 Supreme Court decision legalizing abortion, is now pro-life. She declared these memorable words:

> I am Norma McCorvey. I became known as Jane Roe on January 22, 1973, when the U.S. Supreme Court released the *Roe v. Wade* decision, which created a woman's "right to abortion." I am now a child of God, a new creature in Christ; I am forgiven and redeemed. Today, I publicly recant my involvement in the tragedy of abortion. I humbly ask forgiveness of the millions of women and unborn babies who have experienced the violence of abortion. In this place of healing, the National Memorial for the Unborn, I stand with those who honor the worth of every unborn child as created in the image of God. I will strive, in the name of Jesus, to end this holocaust.

God creates every human in His own image and views every life as worthy of salvation. Let's make God's view of abortion our own view as well.

Questions to Consider and Discuss:

1. Were you surprised to learn that abortion was illegal in ancient societies? In what ways do you think our society is advancing, and in what ways do you see it declining into paganism?

2. Pick a statement to discuss further in class:
   a. The mother's womb has become the baby's tomb.
   b. Regardless of what has been declared legal by human governments, God's Word trumps every court decision.
   c. Jesus said, "Ye are they which justify yourselves before men; but God knoweth your hearts: for that which is highly esteemed among men is abomination in the sight of God" (Luke 16:15).
   d. "Woe unto them that call evil good, and good evil" (Isaiah 5:20).
   e. In our "Christian nation," a baby is murdered every thirty seconds around the clock, seven days a week, year in and year out!
   f. If a "Vietnam Memorial wall" listing the names of the children killed by abortion since 1973 were built, it would be about 60 miles long.
   g. The average abortionist brings in a minimum of $372,000.
   h. Seventeen states use public funds to pay for abortions for poor women.
   i. The *New York Times* called abortion a "tough thing for gynecologists" and said the emotions it arouses are so strong that doctors "don't talk to each other about" it.
   j. "Cursed be he that taketh reward to slay an innocent person" (Deuteronomy 27:25).
   k. "They can be abstractly in favor of abortion rights, but they sure don't want to see what an eighteen-week abortion looks like."
   l. God creates every human in his own image and views every life as worthy of salvation.

3. Which of the following statements surprises you the most? Comment on it.
   a. America's abortion policy is the most liberal in the western world.
   b. Worldwide, there are approximately 126,000 abortions conducted each day. In the U.S., there are approximately 3,753 abortions a day.
   c. Each year in America, 2 out of every 100 women aged 15–44 have an abortion; 48 percent of them have had at least one previous abortion and 61 percent have had a previous birth.

d. In the U.S., 43 percent of women will have had at least one abortion by age 45.

e. Except for biopsies, abortion is the most common surgical procedure performed in the U.S.

f. On average an abortion costs $372.

g. One child in three dies by abortion in the U.S.

h. The most dangerous place for a child in America is inside the child's mother.

i. The casualties of our wars put together are fewer than the casualties from abortion in a single year.

j. Women having abortions "are never allowed to look at the ultrasound because we knew that if they so much as heard the heart beat, they wouldn't want to have an abortion."

4. Why do you think the number of abortion providers in the U.S. is decreasing?

5. If abortion is "after-the-fact birth control," what steps can churches take to help prevent the unwanted pregnancies that often lead to abortion?

6. Do you feel that the church is doing all it should to teach on abstinence and moral issues?

7. Role play: Read Proverbs 1:11–29 and consider a group of doctors trying to persuade another to join them in opening an abortion clinic.

CHAPTER SEVEN

ABORTION WRONGS

W e hear a lot about "abortion rights." We should be discussing "abortion wrongs." Much misinformation is distributed on this subject. Let us consider some of the common arguments for abortion.

ABORTION RIGHTS?

A woman's right over her body. We are blessed to live in a country with a *Bill of Rights*. Each person is entitled to privacy, liberty, and life. Women should be allowed to make decisions about their own bodies, of course, as should men. However, "personal rights end when exercise of them could and does lead to endangering one's own life and the lives of others (i.e. drunk driving and drug addiction, murder, endangering another's life through negligence)."[1] When a woman gets pregnant, she becomes responsible for another body. The *Golden Rule* applies in this situation: "Therefore all things whatsoever ye would that men should do to you, do ye even so to them: for this is the law and the prophets" (Matthew 7:12; cf. Philippians 2:4). Would I want to be aborted? Ronald Reagan was right when he said, "I have noticed that all those who are in favor of abortion were born."

A political cartoon pointed out the inconsistency and the real problem behind abortion:

First Frame: "He kissed me and I melted."
Second Frame: "My heart pounded at his touch."
Third Frame: "His embrace sent blood coursing through my veins."

Fourth Frame: "I was overcome with passion. I couldn't refuse."

Fifth Frame: "Well, now I'm pregnant and I want an abortion."

Last Frame: "After all, a woman should have control over her body."[2]

If there is irresponsibility prior to pregnancy, the chances are greatly increased that there will be irresponsibility afterwards.[3]

Some argue that though the baby is human and alive, he or she does not have the same rights that a mother has. Some even use Exodus 21:22 to say God sanctions such an idea. Actually, this text teaches the opposite (cf. Exodus 21:28–37). Moses wrote, "If men strive, and hurt a woman with child, so that her fruit depart from her, and yet no mischief follow: he shall be surely punished, according as the woman's husband will lay upon him; and he shall pay as the judges determine" (Exodus 21:22). The phrase "no mischief follow" means that the baby is born prematurely but is healthy. But if "mischief followed," that is, the baby was injured or dead, then punishment was to be exacted according to the injury: eye for an eye, tooth for tooth, life for life.

Mother's life endangered. This is very rare; with medical advancements, abortion can almost always be avoided. Dr. C. Everett Koop, former U.S. Surgeon General, said:

> Protection of the life of the mother as an excuse for an abortion is a smoke screen. In my 36 years of pediatric surgery, I have never known of one instance where the child had to be aborted to save the mother's life. The doctor will either induce labor or perform a Caesarean section. His intention is to save the life of both the mother and the baby. The baby's life is never willfully destroyed because the mother's life is in danger. (http://www.lamblion.com/articles/other/social/SI-21.php)

Dr. R. J. Hefferman said, "Anyone who performs a therapeutic abortion (for physical disease) is either ignorant of modern methods of treating the complications of pregnancy, or is unwilling to take the time to use them."[4]

In those extremely rare cases when a choice must be made between a mother's life and the child's (for example, tubal pregnancies), what should be done? The dilemma is the same faced when two lives are jeopardized in a fire or flood. If both cannot be saved, who is to live? Obviously, this would be a difficult choice. In the case of choosing between a mother and a child, the decision would be made by loving parents after much prayer. Abortion is justifiable in such a case as an act of self-defense. This is not an argument for abortion on demand, which would be like casting an unwanted child back into the fire or water!

Skyrocketing child abuse. Child abuse is a horrible crime. It needs to be addressed; violators need to face severe punishments. But is the answer to child abuse killing unwanted children? Is not this the ultimate form of child abuse?

Actually, since abortion was legalized, child abuse has climbed by at least 500 percent, even though we have prevented the birth of more than 40,000,000 unwanted children.

There is much we still do not know about the sick psychology that leads to child abuse. One thing does stand out, however: prenatally, often these were not unwanted pregnancies, they were super-wanted pregnancies. A landmark study was done at the University of Southern California. Edward Lenoski, Professor of Pediatrics and Emergency Medicine at the University of Southern California School of Medicine, studied 674 consecutive battered children who were brought to the in- and out-patient departments of a medical center. He was the first to go to the parents and study to what extent they wanted and planned the pregnancy.

To his surprise, he found that 91 percent were planned and wanted, compared to 63 percent for the control groups nationally. Further, the mothers had begun wearing, on average, pregnancy clothes at 114 days, compared to 171 days in the control, and the fathers named the boys after themselves 24 percent of the time, compared to 4 percent for the control groups.[5]

If the parents wanted children, what led to the abuse? The parents commonly "grew up in a hostile environment, and were themselves abused. When the children fail to satisfy their [unrealistic, neurotic expectations of perfection] emotional needs, the parents react with the same violence they experienced as children."[6]

What about rape? For a man to force a woman is an unspeakable crime. Every woman fears rape above nearly any other evil. Every husband and father of a daughter abhors the thought of those under his care being violated. Such cowardly evil boils the blood of every true man and turns the stomach of any normal person. Such selfishness shows a heart so small and closed that it hardly qualifies to say it is made in God's image.

Whenever abortion is argued, invariably a pro-abortion speaker will say, "If you outlaw abortion, then rape victims would have no recourse but to bear a rapist's child." Is this a valid reason to keep abortion legal for any woman for any reason? Let us consider three introduction points and a brief discussion of each.

First, let us define rape. Rape is the forcible imposition of a man on a woman for sexual intercourse. This study is discussing assault forcible rape, not marital rape, or remorse over consensual sex. Whether a rape occurs behind the bushes or on a date, the victim should report it to the police and file charges. (College students, are you listening?)[7]

Second, it is interesting that the percentage of rape abortions is actually less than the percentage of unwanted babies conceived outside of marriage. Fifty-one percent of unmarried women who become pregnant with boyfriends have abortions; fewer than half of rape pregnancies are aborted. The rest carry the baby to term and give the child up for adoption or opt to keep the child. In one study of thirty-seven rape pregnancies, twenty-eight carried to term.[8]

Third, stiffer laws and better enforcement provide more protection for women than abortion rights. Sex criminals should face the quick and severe wrath of an angry society and government (Romans 13:1–5); this would go far in preventing these tragedies (Ecclesiastes 8:11).

Focusing on abortion as the easy solution to a traumatic problem, abortionists fail to explain that pregnancy resulting from rape is both uncommon and unlikely. Furthermore, advising rape victims to get abortions is unwise and unfair. Consider the facts.

Pregnancy after rape is uncommon. The rape argument for abortion is a smoke-screen used to prejudice undecided minds. These situations make up a very small percentage of abortions in the United States. The Alan Guttmacher Institute, a research arm of Planned Parenthood, completed a survey of 1,900 women who had abortions. Their reasons included the following:

- 21% said they were not ready for the responsibility.
- 21% said they could not afford the baby.
- 16% were concerned about how a child would change their lives.
- 12% blamed a relationship problem.
- 11% felt they were not mature enough.
- 8% said they had all the children they wanted.
- 1% were the result of rape and incest.

Keep in mind that this one-percent figure is from a pro-choice source. According to AGI data, about 14,000 women have abortions each year because they became pregnant after rape or incest. This is out of a total of 1,370,000 abortions.[9] It is possible that the true number is even smaller. In many cases, there is social pressure to claim rape to justify a decision to abort. Forty-three percent of women obtaining abortions identify themselves as Protestant and 27 percent as Catholic. Both groups are historically anti-abortion, but often give exceptions in cases of rape or incest.

That false claims of rape are made is commonly understood in discussion of the abortion issue. The story of Jane Roe, of the infamous *Roe v. Wade* decision, is a case in point. In the early 1970s, Norma McCorvey (her real name) fabricated a story about being gang raped at a circus, mistakenly thinking this would permit her to obtain a legal abortion in Texas. In 1987, she revealed that the baby was actually conceived "through what I thought was love."[10] She had made up the rape story.

Another case is Pennsylvania's Medicaid program. Originally, abortions were funded for women who claimed they had been raped, without requiring reporting to a law enforcement agency. Abortion clinic personnel issued thinly veiled invitations for women to simply say they had been raped. Since they did not have to prove it, and no one would arrest the "rapists," many took advantage of the offer. Based on unsubstantiated claims, the state funded an average of 36 abortions a month. In 1988, when the legislature added a requirement for reporting the rape to a law enforcement agency, the average dropped to less than three abortions per month.

Pregnancy after rape is unlikely. The likelihood of becoming pregnant from rape is, thankfully, very low. Pregnancy occurs in only about one in 4,000 rapes.[11] (Normal pregnancy rates are about 1 in 1,000 copulations.) There are physical reasons for this low rate. It is likely because of timing—not during the three days a month a woman is likely to get pregnant—and because the rapist often does not finish the sex act. Also, some women who are raped are sterile, are on contraception, or are before or after child-bearing years.

Emotional reasons also affect one's ability to become pregnant. A rape victim rarely gets pregnant because conception is unlikely during psychic trauma. Our benevolent Creator so made the feminine reproductive system that she rarely conceives under stress. To get pregnant and stay pregnant, a woman's body must produce a very sophisticated mixture of hormones. Hormone production is controlled by a part of the brain which is easily influenced by emotions. Every woman is aware that stress and emotional factors can alter her menstrual cycle. There is no greater emotional trauma that can be experienced by a woman than an assault rape. This can radically upset her possibility of ovulation, fertilization, implantation, and even nurturing a pregnancy.

Counseling abortion after rape is unwise. What advice should be given a rape victim in the most traumatic time of her life? In most cases involving a pregnancy, the victim did not report to a hospital for help; she kept it to herself. For several weeks, she thought of little else. Now, she has finally asked for help, has shared her upsetting story, and is in a very vulnerable, frightening situation. Her main questions are: "What should I do now? Should I carry the baby or have an abortion?" Is abortion her best option or, as many see it, her only option?

When pregnancy follows rape, victims need moral support, financial help, frank understanding, sheltering by caring family and friends, and assistance from a fair government. Abortion should not be counseled.

Why? First, two wrongs do not make a right. There is no way to ignore God's words: "No murderer hath eternal life abiding in him" (1 John 3:15). The trauma has already occurred. She has been raped. She will live with that fact regardless of whether or not she has an abortion. She has been the victim of one violent act. Should we now ask her to be a party to a second violent act?

Many would counsel her to return violence (killing a baby) for violence (rape) (cf. Matthew 5:38–41). Will she be able to live comfortably with the memory that she had an abortion? Would she ultimately be more at peace with herself if she could remember that, even though she became pregnant unwillingly, she nevertheless solved her problem by being unselfish, by returning love for hate? Compare this memory with the woman who can only look back and say, "I killed my baby." One study concluded, "We found the rape experience is forgotten (what he did), replaced by remembering the abortion, because it is what she did."[12]

Second, abortion is unwise because abortion can be physically dangerous to the mother. Unsuccessful second pregnancies occur more than twice as often among those who have had abortions. Dr. John Wilke explains that in the first and third trimesters, a woman who has had a previous abortion is two times more likely to have a miscarriage, and in the second trimester is ten times more likely.[13] Further, her baby is two times more likely to die after birth than a baby of a mother who has not had an abortion. Other dangers include premature births, tubal pregnancies, loss of interest in sexual activity, damage to the reproductive organs, intractable hemorrhages, pelvic pain, infertility, severe emotional and psychiatric problems, and even death.[14]

Abortion is also dangerous to the mother emotionally. Many feel serious emotional pain after having had an abortion. In recent years, it has become clear that women who have abortions after rape can suffer from Post-Abortion Syndrome (PAS). A national research project on PAS included these statements from women who had obtained abortions (reason for abortion not given):

- "It affected my relationship with my children because I emotionally pushed them away—I felt I didn't deserve them."
- "I would go to the cemetery wondering what they did with my baby."
- "Initially I also felt a sense of relief that it was all over. But it was a strange brand of relief that did everything relief should, except make me feel any better."

A woman who aborted a "rape" baby can carry the same burdens of guilt, denial, and depression that a woman who aborted a "love" baby often does. Why is this? At least two dynamics seem obvious. Rape was something done to her. She was not responsible. She was the innocent victim of another's violence. By contrast, the abortion was done by her. She agreed to it. It was her decision to solicit the second act of violence. And she comes to see it as her own unborn child. The newly-conceived baby is certainly the "rapist's child," but he or she is also her child—half of the new baby's genetic material came from her.[15]

Counseling abortion after rape is unfair. Let's look at it this way. Do we punish other criminals by killing their children? The innocent baby committed no crime. He should not bear punishment for the crimes of his father (Ezekiel 18:4, 20). Just as there are lasting emotional consequences of this violent crime, when pregnancy follows, there are physical consequences as well. Our philosophy of judgment seems terribly unequal at this point. Our courts have declared capital punishment for rapists to be cruel and inhumane. The guilty father only gets a few years' punishment, and often gets nothing but a slap on the wrist. But we execute capital punishment on the innocent baby!

There is no happy solution to every problem pregnancy, but evidence of concern from society for both mother and child, positive support, and financial assistance are more humane. It may surprise you that a rape victim's chief complaint is not that she got pregnant. The most common complaint is "how other people treat her." The most frequently cited factors that make it difficult to continue her pregnancy are others' opinions, attitudes, and beliefs; in other words, how her family, friends, and associates treat her.[16] This should cause us to reflect and consider. Do we try to understand her trauma, and love and support her more because of it? Or do we avoid her because we don't know what to say? Do we act as if it was partly her fault or as if she just made it up? If all such victims were given generous love and support, perhaps many more would carry their babies to term.[17]

Adoption, rather than abortion, is the best option. God gives strength to get through troubled times (1 Corinthians 10:13; Philippians 4:13). We must let rape victims know that it is acceptable to feel that they cannot cope with rearing a child fathered by a rapist. The baby need not grow up feeling unwanted. Innumerable arms are outstretched, aching for a child to love. Adoption agencies across the nation have long lists of those waiting for babies.

Does anyone win after a rape? Once, after a radio program answering questions about rape, an author was called to the phone. He heard a woman's voice say,

> You were talking about me. You see, I am the product of rape. An intruder forced his way into my parents' house, tied up my father and, with him watching, raped my mother. I was conceived that night. Everyone advised an abortion. The local doctors and hospital were willing. My father, however, said, "Even though not mine, that is a child and I will not allow it to be killed!" I don't know how many times that, as I lay secure in the loving arms of my husband, I have thanked God for my wonderful Christian father.

And so, does anyone win? Yes, the baby does.

What about incest? Incest is intercourse between a girl or woman and a close male relative. In the Old Testament a man was forbidden to have intercourse with his mother, stepmother, half-sister, granddaughter, stepsister, aunt, uncle's wife, daughter-in-law, sister-in-law, stepdaughter, step-granddaughter, or mother-in-law. Under Jewish law, such a man was "cut off in the sight of their people" (Leviticus 20:17).

Incest is seldom reported; when reported, it is difficult to prove. It usually involves an evil man, who God says is worthy of death (Romans 1:32), and a cowardly mother who knows but can't or won't admit it is happening, and an exploited child.

Thankfully, pregnancy is not very common.[18] When pregnancy does occur, it is often an attempt to end the relationship—stop the incest—an attempt to unite mother and daughter, or a way to get out of the house. In a twisted sort of way, however, the father is often a "love object." In one study, only 3 of 13 child-mothers had any negative feelings toward the incestuous father.[19] Most incestuous pregnancies, if not pressured, will not get abortions. "As socially inappropriate as incest and incestuous pregnancies are, their harmful effects depend largely upon reaction of others."[20]

Most pregnancies from incest have a very different dynamic than pregnancy from rape. These are usually counseled in a very different manner. Even strongly pro-abortion counselors, if they approach an incest case professionally, must be absolutely convinced before advising abortion. There are two reasons. One, often the young mother sees it as an assault on her, for she may well be pregnant with a "love object." Two, it may completely fail to solve the original problem. It is unusual for wisdom to dictate anything but adoptive placement of the baby.

A handicapped child. If tests show that an unborn baby is handicapped, some will ask, "Is all human life sacred?" If the answer is yes, then no human baby should be killed. If the answer is no, then the question is, "Who gets to decide which life is sacred and important, and which is not?" From a Christian perspective, it is not in man's prerogative to take what rightly belongs to God. Joseph asked, "Am I in the place of God?" (Genesis 50:19). The question is rhetorical. Its implied answer is, "Of course not!" To terminate a single life is to set up man's wisdom as being superior to God's wisdom. Paul reminded the Corinthians: "The foolishness of God is wiser than men; and the weakness of God is stronger than men" (1 Corinthians 1:25). The meaning: God on His worst day is better than man on his best day.

Many of these abortion decisions are made in second or third trimesters because this is when defects are usually discovered. These abortions are often "partial-birth abortions," which is the "blue flame" of the current red-hot debate. Dr. Bernard Nathanson[21] testified before Congress on reproductive technologies on February 9, 2000. Consider these excerpts from his speech:

> Partial-birth abortion is not an abortion at all. Abortion is defined as the separation of a mother from the fetus before 20 weeks. Most of these so-called operations are performed at 28 to 30 weeks. I happen to know one of the doctors who performs these operations. . . . They are really infanticides. He has told me point-blank that 80 percent of the operations he does are done after 30 weeks when someone, the mother or the doctor, discovers things are not going right with the pregnancy. They do an ultrasound and find a congenitally defective baby . . . and therefore the mother elects to have the procedure done. What I'd advocate is what is done in England by law; that every pregnant woman have an ultrasound at 18 weeks. That may not cut the rate of abortion by much . . . but at least it would cut these so-called partial-birth abortions down, and it leaves the mother more breathing room, more time to make up her mind and it allows more time for us pro-life people to do the appropriate counseling to allow her to carry the pregnancy to term and then have the congenital defect repaired.

We are blessed to live in a time when half of such cases can be corrected. We need to continue to pray that doctors will find ways to cure other children who are born handicapped.

To say that it is moral to kill any baby in the womb is to open the door for more than most abortionists bargain for. Why not kill the defective child after birth? What level of perfection is required before a baby should be allowed to live? All of us have imperfections. Who has the power to decide? The doctor? The parents? A panel of "experts"? Why not wait and ask the child? Dr. C. Everett Koop, prior to becoming Surgeon General of the U.S., did just that. He spent his life as a pediatric surgeon repairing "nature's mistakes." For some children, this meant thirty or more operations. At one reunion of the kids he repaired, with all the pain and therapy this implies, he asked if they had to start over, would they want the surgery again? These young people unanimously said, "Yes."

Most people in education and the media who push for abortion have a basic philosophy that differs from the Christian's worldview. They are humanists; that is, they have an atheistic worldview in which man is his own god (cf. Judges 17:6). Man rules his life and determines his destiny. He is a highly evolved, tool-using animal whose value is measured by his productivity. The unborn is not productive to society, and if he will never be able to function normally, he is undesirable. From a humanist perspective, taking a "useless" life is not immoral; it's practical.

- The Australian ethicist, Peter Singer, wrote that the sanctity-of-life view, the "religious mumbo-jumbo," should be stripped away. "Species membership in Homo-sapiens is not morally relevant." If we "compare a dog or a pig to a severely defective infant," he said, "we often find the non-human to have superior capacities." To Singer, quality of life is the only guide.[22]

- Joseph Fletcher suggested using the I.Q. measurement and allow those with an I.Q. under 20 or perhaps 40 to be declared "non-human."[23]

- They followed Nobel Laureate James Watson, the man who cracked the genetic code. He said, "Because of the present limits of such detection methods, most birth defects are not discovered until birth. If a child were not declared alive until three days after birth, then all parents could be allowed the choice . . . the doctor could allow the child to die, if the parents so choose, and save a lot of misery and suffering."

Save a lot of misery and suffering? Death by starvation, dehydration, and exposure is hardly pain-free. Should we say that Hitler was ahead of his time, or that we have regressed to Naziism?

THE PARADOX OF MODERN THINKING

Save the rivers from industry!
Save the mountains from the strip-mines!
Save the redwoods from the woodsman!
Save the earth from her polluters!
But kill the babies in their mothers.
Save the whooping cranes! Save the wolves!
Save the blackbirds! Save the gators!
But kill the baby (spare the rapist father).
Save the seal pups! Save the fur bearers!
Save the hawks! Save even the vultures and the crows!
But kill the babies at the whim of their mothers.
Save the whales! Save the beaver! Save the snail darter!
Save the murderers, terrorists, and assassins!
But kill the babies, the weak, and the defective.
Kill the unwanted babies! Kill the senile grandfathers!
Kill the deformed and the retarded!
Kill the mentally and terminally ill![24]

Another more practical reason to avoid abortion in such cases is that parents emotionally handle the abortion of a handicapped baby very poorly. One study reported maternal depression of 92 percent and paternal depression of 82 percent, plus a 30 percent incidence of marital separation after the abortion.[25]

SOME HOPEFUL NEWS

The Pro-Life Movement in our country is making progress.

- According to a *USA Today/CNN/Gallup Poll* in May 1999, 16 percent of Americans believe abortion should be legal for any reason at any time during pregnancy, and 55 percent of Americans believe abortion should be legal only to save the life of the mother or in cases of rape or incest.

- According to a *Gallup Poll* in January 2001, people who considered themselves to be pro-life rose from 33 percent to 43 percent in the past five years, and people who considered themselves to be pro-choice declined from 56 percent to 48 percent.

Still, there is much work to be done. John Adams sent a simple letter to the Continental Congress during the battle for independence with three questions:

- Is anyone there?
- Does anyone see?
- Does anyone care?

Martin Niemoller was a preacher of a church in Germany in the 1930s. Eventually, Niemoller became one of the millions of victims arrested and killed in Hitler's concentration camps. Shortly before his death, he wrote:

> In Germany they first came for the Communists, and I didn't speak up because I wasn't a Communist. Then they came for the Jews, and I didn't speak up because I wasn't a Jew. Then they came for the trade unionists, and I didn't speak up because I wasn't a trade unionist. Then they came for the Catholics, and I didn't speak up because I was Protestant. And then they came for me, and by that time no one was left to speak up.

Niemoller learned too late that indifference kills. We can murder by arranging a death, or we can murder by allowing a death (1 John 3:16–18). Is your voice being heard in the abortion battle?[26] Is your vote for pro-choice candidates when pro-life candidates are available? Party loyalty or economic philosophies must take a backseat to moral issues. Solomon's statement needs considering in voting booths: "Righteousness exalteth a nation, but sin is a reproach to any people" (Proverbs 14:34). "Soldiers of Christ arise and put your armor on."

Isaiah urged, "Cry aloud, spare not, lift up thy voice like a trumpet, and declare unto my people their transgressions" (Isaiah 58:1). Abortion is not a right; it is a wrong.

Questions to Consider and Discuss

1. Does the *Golden Rule*, "Therefore all things whatsoever ye would that men should do to you, do ye even so to them: for this is the law and the prophets" (Matthew 7:12), have an application in the abortion discussion?

2. Choose a statement to discuss further in class:
    a. Abortion is not a "right"; it is a "wrong."
    b. "Personal rights end when exercise of them could and does lead to endangering one's own life and the lives of others."
    c. "I have noticed that all those who are in favor of abortion were born" (Ronald Reagan).
    d. If there is irresponsibility prior to pregnancy, the chances are greatly increased there will be irresponsibility afterwards.
    e. "Protection of the life of the mother as an excuse for an abortion is a smoke screen" (Dr. C. Everett Koop).
    f. Fifty-one percent of unmarried women who become pregnant with boyfriends have abortions; fewer than 50 percent of rape pregnancies are aborted.
    g. "No murderer hath eternal life abiding in him" (1 John 3:15).
    h. "We found the rape experience is forgotten (what he did), replaced by remembering the abortion, because it is what she did."
    i. Adoption, rather than abortion, is the best option.
    j. "Righteousness exalteth a nation, but sin is a reproach to any people" (Proverbs 14:34).
    k. "Cry aloud, spare not, lift up thy voice like a trumpet, and declare unto my people their transgressions" (Isaiah 58:1).

3. Has legalized abortion helped limit child abuse?

4. What arguments are made against counseling abortion in cases of rape?

5. In what ways can abortion be dangerous to the mother? Do you think this is made clear by the media and abortion providers to those considering abortion?

6. What is "Post-Abortion Syndrome"?

7. What is the most common complaint of women who have been raped? What can the church do to help?

8. Why do even strongly pro-abortion professional counselors often not advise abortion in cases of incest?

9. Most of those who favor abortion have adopted a humanist worldview. What does this mean?

10. Do you think that doctors are "playing God" when they advise parents to have abortions in cases of handicapped children? How can the church better show Christ's love to handicapped children and their parents?

CHAPTER EIGHT

A HEART THAT DEVISETH WICKED IMAGINATIONS

Proverbs 6:18

The human mind is constantly computing information. Our senses soak up and send our minds a flood of over 100,000,000 bits of data every second. With so many thoughts going through our brains, it stands to reason that we should guard them against evil. David reminded Solomon that "the LORD searcheth all hearts, and understandeth all the imaginations of the thoughts" (1 Chronicles 28:9). Various forms of the word *imagination* are found 35 times in the Bible—31 in the Old Testament; 4 in the New Testament.

The modifier *wicked*—including *wickedness, wickedly*—is found 453 times in the Scriptures. The word used in Proverbs 6:18 (*'aven*) comes from an unused root perhaps meaning "to pant," and hence means "to exert oneself." Man's capacity for wickedness seems to surprise even his Creator. God told Ezekiel: "Go in, and behold the wicked abominations that they do here. So I went in and saw" (Ezekiel 8:9–10).

The Scriptures give three examples of devising wicked imaginations that still tempt us today: plotting against others, revenge, and pornography.

THE TEMPTATION OF PLOTTING AGAINST OTHERS

The heart is the seat of the emotions. If a man has a spirit of compassion and kindness, we say his heart is in the right place. One who is sad is called heartsick. Likewise, someone who cherishes feelings of bitterness might be said to have an ailing heart. Solomon states that "a sound heart is the life of the flesh: but envy the rottenness of the bones" (Proverbs 14:30).

God said, "And let none of you imagine evil in your hearts against his neighbour; and love no false oath: for all these are things that I hate, saith the LORD" (Zechariah 8:17). These plots might involve:

- Taking another's property or position (Genesis 27:5–17; 1 Kings 21:1–16);
- Rape (2 Samuel 13:1–15);
- Hate crimes/persecution (Esther 7:3–6; Daniel 6:1–8; Acts 23:12–22); or,
- Revenge (Genesis 27:41–45).

WHEN DOES THE WICKED MAN DEVISE HIS EVIL PLANS?

"He deviseth mischief upon his bed; he setteth himself in a way that is not good; he abhorreth not evil" (Psalm 36:4). "Woe to them that devise iniquity, and work evil upon their beds! when the morning is light, they practice it, because it is in the power of their hand" (Micah 2:1).

Solomon spoke of another who "deviseth mischief continually" (Proverbs 6:14). This implies that the wicked man had a back-up plan for evil. If one plot failed, he formed another; when one scheme succeeded, he at once set to work at a fresh one on a different person.

WHAT ARE THE CONSEQUENCES OF WICKED IMAGINATIONS?

Sadness. "Deceit is in the heart of them that imagine evil: but to the counsellors of peace is joy" (Proverbs 12:20). This is a contrasting proverb, what scholars call "antithetical parallelism." Since those who counsel peace receive joy, the implication is that those who counsel evil receive sadness.

Scattering. "He hath showed strength with his arm; he hath scattered the proud in the imagination of their hearts" (Luke 1:51). This may be a reference to the people at the tower of Babel (Genesis 11:1–8).

Brokenness. "Therefore shall his calamity come suddenly; suddenly shall he be broken without remedy" (Proverbs 6:15). God promises that this person will be like a potter's vessel which, once broken, cannot be mended (cf. Psalm 2:9; Revelation 2:27). "How long will ye imagine mischief against a man? ye shall be slain all of you: as a bowing wall shall ye be, and as a tottering fence" (Psalm 62:3).

Separation. "But became vain in their imaginations, and their foolish heart was darkened . . . Wherefore God also gave them up" (Romans 1:21–24).

Rejection. "Casting down imaginations,[1] and every high thing that exalteth itself against the knowledge of God, and bringing into captivity every thought to the obedience of Christ" (2 Corinthians 10:5).

WHAT BIBLE CHARACTERS FACED ENEMIES WITH WICKED IMAGINATIONS?

Job's friends imagined false accusations against him (Job 6:24–27; 21:27). Haman schemed to injure Mordecai (Esther 3). King David had much trouble with those who intended evil against him. Note a sampling of his writings on the subject:

- "They imagined[2] a mischievous device, which they are not able to perform" (Psalm 21:11).

- "They also that seek after my life lay snares for me: and they that seek my hurt speak mischievous things, and imagine deceits all the day long" (Psalm 38:12).

- "Deliver me, O LORD, from the evil man: preserve me from the violent man; which imagine mischiefs in their heart; continually are they gathered together for war. They have sharpened their tongues like a serpent; adders' poison is under their lips. Selah. Keep me, O LORD, from the hands of the wicked; preserve me from the violent man; who have purposed to overthrow my goings. The proud have hid a snare for me, and cords; they have spread a net by the wayside; they have set gins for me. Selah. I said unto the LORD, Thou art my God: hear the voice of my supplications, O LORD" (Psalm 140:1–6).

Nehemiah overcame plots against his life and still finished God's work in record time (Nehemiah 4:1–8). Read Lamentations 3:60–61 to see Jeremiah's complaint to God.

God referred to plots against His Son a thousand years before those who would perpetrate them were ever born: "Why do the heathen rage, and the people imagine[3] a vain thing?" (Psalm 2:1). Contextually, this is a prophecy of the plots made against Jesus' life that culminated in His murder (Matthew 21:38; John 11:49–50). The chief priests and scribes—"the people"—held consultations in orchestrating the death of Christ (Mark 11:18; 14:1–5). The Roman soldiers and Herod's men—"the heathen"—mocked and raged against Him.

HOW DID GOD'S SERVANTS HANDLE THEIR ENEMIES' PLOTS?

In David's case, we gain insight in this passage: "But I, as a deaf man, heard not; and I was as a dumb man that openeth not his mouth. Thus I was as a man that heareth not, and in whose mouth are no reproofs. For in thee, O LORD, do I hope: thou wilt hear, O LORD my God" (Psalm 38:13–15).

- David ignored them—as a deaf man;
- David refused to respond to them—as a dumb man;
- David trusted in God to handle them—as an impotent (weak) man.

In Nehemiah's case, he prayed (Nehemiah 4:4), kept doing God's work (4:6), and refused to compromise or to cease working to "dialogue" (6:3).

To fulfill God's purposes, Christ submitted to His enemies "as a lamb dumb before his shearer" (Acts 8:32; Matthew 26:62–63). He went the second mile to express love and forgiveness (Luke 23:34).

THE TEMPTATION OF SEEKING REVENGE

Seeking revenge is another application of the wicked imagination. When someone hurts us physically or emotionally, our first reaction may be to get even.

Jack's mother ran into the bedroom when she heard him scream and found his two-year-old sister pulling his hair. She gently released the little girl's grip and said comfortingly to Jack, "There, there. She didn't mean it. She doesn't know that it hurts." Mom was barely out of the room when the little girl screamed. Rushing back, she said, "What happened?"

"She knows now," little Jack explained. That's what the natural man—the immature person—does. Aristotle said, "Men regard it as their right to return evil for evil—and if they cannot, they feel they have lost their liberty."[4]

WHAT DOES A SPIRITUALLY MATURE PERSON DO?

When asked what they would try to do when wronged, American adults chose forgiveness over revenge six to one. A Gallup Poll found that 48 percent would "try to forgive" while only 8 percent would "try to get even." Other responses: discuss the problem (48 percent), overlook the offense (45 percent), pray for comfort and guidance (27 percent), and pray for the offender (25 percent). And while 14 percent admitted they would hold resentment inside, 9 percent said they would try to do something nice for the one who hurt them.[5]

We can resist the temptation to seek revenge by choosing positive reactions to our enemies.

Refuse to nurse a perceived wrong. The old Chinese proverb, "If thine enemy wrong thee, buy each of his children a drum," is bad advice for a Christian. Yet it is the response the world applauds. Three burly fellows on huge motorcycles pulled up to a highway cafe where a truck driver, just a little guy, was perched on a stool quietly eating his lunch. As the three fellows came in, they spotted him, grabbed his food away from him, and laughed in his face. The truck driver said nothing. He got up, paid for his food, and walked out. One of the three bikers, unhappy that they had not succeeded in provoking a fight, commented to the waitress: "Boy, he sure wasn't much of a man, was he?"

The waitress replied, "Well, I guess not." Then, looking out the window, she added, "I guess he's not much of a truck driver, either. He just ran over three motorcycles."[6]

Francis Bacon (1561–1626) said, "A man that studieth revenge keeps his own wounds green, which otherwise would heal and do well."[7] Moses' Law said, "Thou shalt not avenge" (Leviticus 19:18). Henry Ward Beecher (1813–1887) astutely noted, "'I can forgive, but I cannot forget,' is only another way of saying, 'I will not forgive.'" Publilius Syrus (first century B.C.) said, "It is foolish to punish your neighbor by fire when you live next door." Jesus said, "No man, having put his hand to the plow, and looking back, is fit for the kingdom of God" (Luke 9:62). He also taught us the absolute necessity of forgiving when He taught us to pray for forgiveness based on our willingness to forgive those who sin against us (Matthew 6:12, 14–15).

Trust in God to fix things. "Vengeance is mine; I will repay, saith the Lord" (Romans 12:19). Abe Lemmons was asked if he was bitter at Deloss Dodds, the Texas Athletic Director who fired him as the Longhorn's basketball coach. He replied, "Not at all, but I plan to buy a glass-bottomed car so I can watch the look on his face when I run over him."[8] We don't have to plan revenge; we have a Protector who always does what is right. Let's leave settling accounts to Him.

Rise above it. An eagle knows when a storm is approaching long before it breaks. It will fly to some high spot and wait for the winds to come. When the storm hits, it sets its wings so that the wind will lift it above the storm. While the storm rages below, the bird soars above it. The eagle does not escape the storm; it uses it.

Isaiah compares people to eagles:

> Even the youths shall faint and be weary, and the young men shall utterly fall: but they that wait upon the LORD shall renew their strength; they shall mount up with wings as eagles; they shall run, and not be weary; and they shall walk, and not faint (Isaiah 40:30–31).

We can ride the winds of the storm that bring sickness, tragedy, failure, and disappointment into our lives. We can soar above the storm. It is not the burdens of life that weigh us down, it is the way we handle them.

When we get even with people, that is literally what we are doing—becoming "even," that is, descending to their level and losing the moral advantage we had.[9] Francis Bacon said, "In taking revenge, a man is but even with his enemy; but in passing it over, he is superior."[10] Juvenal said, "Revenge is the poor delight of little minds."[11]

Most of us would do well to read often and carefully the teaching of the Master:

> Ye have heard that it hath been said, Thou shalt love thy neighbour, and hate thine enemy. But I say unto you, Love your enemies, bless them that curse you, do good to them that hate you, and pray for them which despitefully use you, and persecute you; that ye may be the children of your Father which is in heaven: for he maketh his sun to rise on the evil and on the good, and sendeth rain on the just and on the unjust. For if ye love them which love you, what reward have ye? do not even the publicans the same? And if ye salute your brethren only, what do ye more than others? do not even the publicans so? Be ye therefore perfect, even as your Father which is in heaven is perfect (Matthew 5:43–48).

Get on with life. Paul wrote,

> Brethren, I count not myself to have apprehended: but this one thing I do, forgetting those things which are behind, and reaching forth unto those things which are before, I press toward the mark for the prize of the high calling of God in Christ Jesus (Philippians 3:13–14).

George Herbert said, "Living well is the best revenge."[12] It costs more to revenge injuries than to bear them. "Never does the human soul appear so strong as when it foregoes revenge and dares to forgive an injury."[13]

Go the second mile. Alexander C. Dejong said,

> To forgive someone involves three things. First, it means to forego the right of striking back. One rejects the urge to repay gossip with gossip and a bad turn with a worse turn. Second, it means replacing the feeling of resentment and anger with good will, a love which seeks the other's welfare, not harm. Third, it means the forgiving person takes concrete steps to restore good relations."[14]

Someone expanded on Bacon's statement by observing, "Doing an injury puts you below your enemy; revenging one makes you even with him; forgiving it sets you above him" (see Matthew 18:21–22; Luke 10:25–37; 23:33–34).[15]

Bitterness brings pain to other people, but it leaves its worst scars in the one who harbors the bitterness. On an old *Amos 'n Andy* television program, Andy was angry. A big man slapped Andy across the chest every time they met, until Andy finally had enough of it. He told Amos, "I'm going to get revenge. I put a stick of dynamite in my vest pocket. The next time he slaps me on the chest, he's going to get his hand blown off." But Andy did not consider that the dynamite would blow his own heart out.[16]

Revenge may hurt the other person, but it always blows our own heart out. Francis Bacon said, "Men must not turn into bees and kill themselves in stinging others." The Chinese have a proverb, "He who seeks revenge, digs two graves." On the other hand, there is healing in cherishing the constructive emotions of hope, peace, love, kindness, and trust. The healing processes have a much better chance to work in the body of one who is tranquil in mind and who refuses to harbor a grudge. Jesus prayed, "Father, forgive them; for they know not what they do" (Luke 23:34).

THE TEMPTATION OF PORNOGRAPHY

The depraved heart is also seen in those who publish, peddle, and purchase pornography. We are fed a constant diet of what we might call muted pornography. Immodest clothing and lascivious behavior are everywhere—from billboards to television to magazines to songs to books.

This is the tip of the iceberg protruding from an erotic underworld. The pornography industry is exploding in the United States:

- There are now more outlets for hard-core pornography in the United States than McDonald's restaurants.[17]

- The United States is the world's leading producer of pornography, producing hard-core videos at the rate of 150 new titles a week.[18]

- Annual rentals and sales of adult videos and DVDs top $4 billion, with the industry producing 11,000 titles each year—an amount more than 20 times as many as Hollywood.[19]

- According to *US News and World Report*, the pornography industry takes in more than $8 billion a year, which is more than rock and country music, and more than all Broadway productions, theater, ballet, jazz, and classical music combined.

- *The Wall Street Journal* estimated that total revenues from pornography exceed the revenues for any professional sport.[20]

- Americans spend more than $8 billion annually on hard-core videos, peep shows, live sex acts, adult cable, sexual devices, computer porn, and sex magazines—an amount much larger than Hollywood's annual domestic combined box office receipts.[21]

- Every night, between 9:00 p.m. and 1:00 a.m., a quarter of a million Americans pick up the phone and dial a number for commercial telephone sex. Americans spend between $750 million and $1 billion annually on telephone sex.[22]

- *Playboy's* website, with free glimpses of its playmates, averages about five million hits a day.[23]

- General Motors, the world's largest company, sells more graphic sex films every year than does Larry Flynt, owner of Hustler. The 8.7 million who subscribe to DirecTV, a GM subsidiary, buy $200 million a year in pay-per-view sex movies.[24]

- Long-distance carriers (including AT&T), cable companies (including Time Warner and Tele-Communications, Inc.), and hotel chains (including Marriott, Hyatt, and Holiday Inn) earn millions of dollars each year by supplying in-room pornographic movies to their guests.[25]

- In one year, Americans spent more than $150 million ordering adult movies on pay-per-view.

- The term "sex" was the most popular term people searched for on the Internet, consisting of 1 of every 300 terms. People used this search term more than the following eight terms combined: "games," "music," "travel," "jokes," "cars," "jobs," "weather," and "health." The term "porn" (including variations) was the fourth most popular search term. Also in the top 20 were "nude/s," "xxx," "playboy," and "erotic stories" (including "erotica").[26]

Needless to say, there is plenty of opportunity for the sin of lust available to everyone (cf. James 1:14–15). We must learn to control our thoughts, or our thoughts will come to control us (Deuteronomy 4:15; Proverbs 25:28; Galatians 6:8; 1 Peter 2:11). Temptation seldom breaks down the front door of the conscience; it usually just quietly enters the back door of the mind.

GUARD YOUR HEART

An individual may suffer the loss of other organs, but no one can sustain the failure of a heart. In a biological sense—and a spiritual sense—it is good advice to "keep thy heart with all diligence; for out of it are the issues of life" (Proverbs 4:23). Our word *brain* is not used in the Old Testament; the word *heart* refers to the center of intellectual activity. A man's physical and spiritual health depend in large part upon the condition of his heart—mind.

Our hearts can get dirty just like our hands. "O Jerusalem, wash thine heart from wickedness, that thou mayest be saved. How long shall thy vain thoughts lodge within thee?" (Jeremiah 4:14; cf. Ephesians 2:1–3; Titus 3:3). Job wondered, "How much more abominable and filthy is man, which drinketh iniquity like water?" (Job 15:16). God Himself said, "For the imagination of man's heart is evil from his youth" (Genesis 8:21).

The wise man said, "Lo, this only have I found, that God hath made man upright; but they have sought out many inventions" (Ecclesiastes 7:29). On a bit more cynical day, he expressed it this way: "This is an evil among all things that are done under the sun, that there is one event unto all: yea, also the heart of the sons of men is full of evil, and madness is in their heart while they live, and after that they go to the dead" (Ecclesiastes 9:3). Jeremiah added: "The heart is deceitful above all things, and desperately wicked: who can know it?" (Jeremiah17:9). The Lord Jesus said, "For out of the heart proceed evil thoughts, murders, adulteries, fornications, thefts, false witness, blasphemies" (Matthew 15:19). It is an ugly brood that comes out of the human heart when it gives in to wicked imaginations.

WHERE DO I DRAW THE LINE?

There is no sin in appreciating someone's beauty in a general sense—"He's a handsome guy"; "She's pretty"—but it becomes lust when one starts to mentally undress, compare, and visualize an encounter. Solomon instructed his son not to "lust after" a woman's beauty "in his heart" (Proverbs 6:25). Sex does not begin in the bedroom or the back seat of a car. It begins in the mind. That is where we must erect our battleworks in the fight with Satan.

Solomon draws the line at lust. *Lust*[27] here literally means to see a woman as a "delectable thing"; it refers to "a burning desire for intimacies with her." The admonition is a warning to stop the very first step toward impure desires. In the context of Solomon's warning, a naive young man saw himself on the verge of satisfying his curiosity about what happens in sexual relations. He watches a loose woman and thinks about what it would be like to have sex. An older man sees the same woman and wonders what it would be like to have sex *with her*. Each undresses her with his eyes and takes home the mental images. Both muse over them while lying in bed and daydream of her while going about their routines at work or school.

These activities are nothing less than sexual foreplay. The battleground for remaining pure in body is remaining pure in mind. To harbor unchaste thoughts and feelings in one's heart is to be guilty of adultery in the heart before God. James explained how sin develops: "A man is tempted, when he is drawn away by his own lust, and enticed" (James 1:14–15). The pure, holy, and undefiled Lord Jesus (Hebrews 7:26) who "knew no sin" (2 Corinthians 5:21) said, "Whosoever looketh on a woman to lust after her hath committed adultery with her already in his heart" (Matthew 5:28). It was lust in Amnon's heart that caused him to rape his half-sister Tamar (2 Samuel 13:1–14).

WHAT ARE SOME GUIDELINES?

- To keep a pure mind, we must put on the whole armor of God (Ephesians 6:11; cf. 2 Chronicles 20:15). Christ gives strength to those who give themselves to Him (Philippians 4:13).

- We must monitor our media intake (Psalm 101:3), and think on good things (Philippians 4:8; Matthew 5:6). We must not feed on evil thoughts (Galatians 5:16; 2 Timothy 2:22). In practical terms, this means we must not read dirty romance novels, watch soaps, or be entertained by sexy pictures on the computer, in magazines, and on television. If necessary, it would be better to cancel cable, magazine subscriptions, and Internet access than to lose one's soul. Just after Jesus condemned lust in the heart He said, "And if thy right eye offend thee, pluck it out, and cast it from thee: for it is profitable for thee that one of thy members should perish, and not that thy whole body should be cast into hell" (Matthew 5:29). This hyperbole is not to be taken literally, but a modern version might read: "If thy cable vision offends you, cut it off and cast it from thee."

- We should ask for God's help (Matthew 6:13; 2 Peter 2:9).

SOME READY REFERENCES
ON PORNOGRAPHY

General:

- Wrong to look on a woman to lust (Matthew 5:27–28).
- After the heart is right with God, good conduct flows from its hidden springs (cf. Matthew 15:19).
- Abstain from appearance of evil (1 Thessalonians 5:22).
- Lascivious; lewd; lustful (Galatians 5:19–21).
- Vile affections (Romans 1:26–32).
- Corrupt, impure, unholy thoughts (Philippians 4:7–8).
- Flee fornication (don't run to it) (1 Corinthians 6:18).
- Do all to God's glory (1 Corinthians 3:17; 10:31).
- Women adorn themselves modestly (1 Timothy 2:9–10).
- Nakedness, or near nakedness, shame in God's sight (Genesis 3:21; 9:21–27).
- Adorn with meek, quiet spirit, not draw attention to outward body (1 Peter 3:3–4).

- Lust brings sin (James 1:14–15).
- Lust destroys soul (1 Peter 2:11).

Dirty Movies/Television:

- Set no wicked thing before eyes (Psalm 101:3).
- Our life is to be living sacrifice, not conformed to world (Romans 12:1–2).
- Adultery, fornication, immodesty, and dancing are projected as acceptable on TV and lessen our distaste for sin (Galatians 5:19–21).
- Language must be pure (Matthew 12:34–37). This forbids sexual innuendoes, which are "verbal porn."
- Steals time from serving God (2 Peter 3:18; Ephesians 5:16).

IDOLATRY AND IMMORAL WICKEDNESS

Following the word *imagination* further through the Bible shows the Holy Spirit applies it to idolatry and moral lapses in many contexts.

- Adam lived long enough to see wickedness take deep root on earth: "Every imagination[28] of the thoughts of his heart was only evil continually" (Genesis 6:5). The wicked imaginations in this context seem to have two fruits: violence and forsaking God's way on the earth (Genesis 6:11–12).

- A little later, the people imagined to build a city and a tower to the heavens (Genesis 11:6). The wickedness here is pride ("make us a name") and disobeying God's command. Jehovah had commanded them to "fill the earth" (Genesis 1:28; 9:1, 7) and they had determined not to be "scattered" (11:4).

- In the Law of Moses, God warned of the man who would walk in the "imagination of his heart" and told the punishment he would face (Deuteronomy 29:19). The wickedness here is idolatry (29:18), denying God's threats, and drunkenness (29:19). Moses taught Israel a song as a warning to future generations about wicked imaginations (Deuteronomy 31:20–22). Idols in the Old Testament are often called "images" (e.g., Genesis 31:19, 34), since man "imagined" them. God said to Ezekiel, "Son of man, hast thou seen what the ancients of the house of Israel do in the dark, every man in the chambers of his imagery? for they say, The LORD seeth us not; the LORD hath forsaken the earth" (Ezekiel 8:12).

- "The wicked in his pride doth persecute the poor: let them be taken in the devices that they have imagined" (Psalm 10:2). The wickedness associated with imagination in this context includes persecuting the poor, pride, boasting, approving of what God hates, and failing to think of God (Psalm 10:3–4).

- "How long will ye imagine mischief against a man? . . . they delight in lies: they bless with their mouth, but they curse inwardly" (Psalm 62:3–4). The wickedness associated with imagination here includes desire to destroy another—jealousy, lying, and hypocrisy.

- "Because that, when they knew God, they glorified him not as God, neither were thankful; but became vain in their imaginations, and their foolish heart was darkened" (Romans 1:21). The wickedness in this context is failing to seek God, glorify God, thank God, and worship God. Idols were substituted for worshipping; perversion replaced God's plan for the family (Romans 1:18–30).

WHERE DO WE PUT OUR ENERGY?

The Hebrew word *deviseth*[29] is from a root meaning "to plow." As a farmer applies himself wholly to the plowing and sowing of his land, so a froward man—perverse, fraudulent—gives himself wholly to iniquity, seeking his harvest of gain or enjoyment. These words picture a man so wicked that he makes committing sin his study. Most people's sins arise from thoughtlessness, weakness, and laziness (Proverbs 6:9–10), but a few make sin their business and apply themselves to it with as much diligence as the merchant gives to his trade or the man of letters to his pursuit of knowledge. This describes some Bible characters (Genesis 6:5; Micah 2:1–3).

By contrast, a righteous man makes it his "study"[30] to be approved of God (2 Timothy 2:15; cf. Hebrews 4:11; 2 Peter 1:10, 15; 3:14). The Bible pictures the importance of entering the kingdom in the most intense way. Men are bidden to "seek" the kingdom (Matthew 6:33; Luke 12:31). Barclay explains that the word is *zetein*, and it could have been translated: "Make the kingdom the object of your endeavor." It is worthy of our most strenuous efforts. Men are said to "press" into the kingdom (Matthew 11:12; Luke 16:16). The word is *biasesthai*, and it is the word used of attackers storming a city. The kingdom of heaven is for people desperately seeking to avoid an eternal separation from God.

To gain citizenship in the kingdom is worth any sacrifice. It is better to surgically cut off any member of the body that would hinder a man from entering the kingdom, than to preserve the body whole and to be shut out of the kingdom (Matthew 5:30; Mark 9:43–48). The kingdom is equated with life itself. If we compare Mark 9:43, 45, and 47, we see that the first two verses speak of life, and the third speaks of the kingdom; the meaning is the same. In the story of the rich young ruler, the young man requests guidance about how to find eternal life (Matthew 19:16; Mark 10:17; Luke 18:18); and when he has made his tragic departure, Jesus' illustration deals with how difficult it is for a rich man to enter the kingdom of God (Matthew 19:23; Mark 10:23; Luke 18:24).

Don't waste your imagination—invest it in propelling you toward heaven.

Questions to Consider and Discuss

1. What four types of plots are mentioned in the Bible?

2. How did David respond to the plots of his enemies?

3. Choose a statement to discuss:
   a. "Men regard it as their right to return evil for evil—and if they cannot, feel they have lost their liberty" (Aristotle).
   b. "If thine enemy wrong thee, buy each of his children a drum" (Chinese proverb).
   c. "Thou shalt not avenge" (Leviticus 19:18).
   d. "It is foolish to punish your neighbor by fire when you live next door" (Publilius Syrus)
   e. "Vengeance is mine; I will repay, saith the Lord" (Romans 12:19).
   f. "Doing an injury puts you below your enemy; revenging one makes you even with him; forgiving it sets you above him."
   g. Our hearts can get dirty just like our hands.
   h. Sex does not begin in the bedroom. It begins in the mind.
   i. "If thy cable vision offends you, cut it off and cast it from thee."
   j. "The kingdom is not for the well-meaning but for the desperate."

4. Which of the following are good ideas when facing the challenge of those who have wronged us?
   a. Try to forgive them.
   b. Try to get even.
   c. Discuss the problem with them.
   d. Overlook the offense.
   e. Pray for comfort and guidance.
   f. Pray for the offender.
   g. Tell others so the same thing won't happen to them.
   h. Try to do something nice for the person.

5. Do you believe that the statement, "I can forgive, but I cannot forget," is only another way of saying, "I will not forgive"?

6. What is meant by the statement: "We are fed a constant diet of muted pornography"? How can Christians best deal with this temptation?

7. Which surprises you the most?
   a. There are more outlets for hard-core pornography in the United States
      than McDonald's restaurants.
   b. The United States is the world's leading producer of pornography, pro-
      ducing hard-core videos at the rate of one hundred fifty new titles a week.
   c. The pornography industry takes in more each year than rock and country
      music, and more than all Broadway productions, theater, ballet, jazz, and
      classical music combined.
   d. The total revenues from pornography exceed the revenues for any profes-
      sional sport.
   e. The term "sex" was the most popular term people searched for on the
      Internet.
8. What are some practical ways to "keep thy heart with all diligence"
   (Proverbs 4:23), as relates to pornography? (Discuss television, magazine,
   and Internet pornography.)

9. At what point does appreciating beauty cross the line to lust?

10. How can women help men obey Matthew 5:28: "Whosoever looketh on a
    woman to lust after her hath committed adultery with her already in his
    heart"?

11. In what ways do those before the Flood (Genesis 6), and those who planned to
    build the Tower of Babel, illustrate "hearts that devise wicked imaginations"?

12. Do you believe that most Christians agree with the statement: "To enter the
    kingdom is worth any sacrifice"? In what ways should we be willing to show it?

CHAPTER NINE

FEET SWIFTLY RUNNING TO MISCHIEF

Proverbs 6:18

Solomon uses the words *feet* and *foot* sixteen times in Proverbs. (The Bible uses the words 326 times.) The wise man counseled, "Ponder the path of thy feet, and let all thy ways be established. Turn not to the right hand nor to the left: remove thy foot from evil" (Proverbs 4:26–27).

God hates "feet swiftly running to mischief" (Proverbs 6:18). In this chapter, let's focus on three examples of Bible characters whose feet ran to mischief: Jonah, the prodigal son, and Satan.

JONAH'S FEET WERE SWIFT IN RUNNING TO MISCHIEF

God told Jonah to go east to preach in Nineveh, the capital of the Assyrian Empire (Jonah 1:1–2). Jonah went west to hide in Tarshish, a city in southwest Spain (1:3). When he got on that boat, he had no idea how far sin was going to take him. God sent a storm and nearly sank the ship. The mariners discovered that Jonah was running from God and threw him overboard.

Stop and think. What was that like? Jonah described it: "For thou hadst cast me into the deep, in the midst of the seas; and the floods compassed me about: all thy billows and thy waves passed over me" (2:3). Drowning is a horrible way to die; to nearly drown is one of the most frightening experiences one can have. Why was Jonah in the water? His feet were swift in running to mischief.

Instead of allowing him to drown, though, the Lord sent a great fish to swallow Jonah (Jonah 1:17). Imagine what it felt like to be swallowed by a fish! Jonah must have been terrified! Why are you in the fish, Jonah? Sin. Down he went to the sea bottom (2:6). Why are you there, Jonah? Sin. For three days, Jonah was in a fish's digestive system! What did it smell like? What did it feel like? "The waters compassed me about, even to the soul: the depth closed me round about, the weeds were wrapped about my head" (2:5).

Finally, God decided class was over and had the fish vomit—God's word (Jonah 2:10)—Jonah out onto land. What did it feel like to be fish vomit? What made Jonah the only person to ever find out? Sin. What did Jonah learn? Sin will take you farther than you want to go.

What does Jonah teach us about taking a trip into sin?

First, it's easy to book passage. Jonah didn't have to wait for a ship going to Tarshish—the devil had it ready for him (Jonah 1:3). Satan keeps boats at the dock for anybody wanting to sail to Tarshish (cf. 2 Corinthians 2:11; 1 Peter 5:8). Sin always lies at the door (Genesis 4:7). It is a wide gate—easy access—that leads to the broad road (Matthew 7:13). If you remain true to God, it won't be because you lacked opportunities to sin; it will be because you had backbone to say no to sin, and faith to say yes to God. What boats does Satan keep ready?

- Teens heading to "Tarshish" find that being underage is no real hindrance to buying beer or cigarettes—an older friend will get it for them or an unscrupulous business man will sell it to them under the table (Proverbs 1:19).

- If men want to tell dirty jokes, they will find that there are plenty of people who will laugh (cf. Romans 1:32).

- If some want to go places and do things their spouses or parents disapprove, they find that friends will lie for them (cf. Ephesians 6:1–4; 2 Timothy 3:2).

- If one wants to do drugs, it is not hard to find someone who can get whatever he wants—for a price. It's so easy to find drugs that about twenty-five teens start using every hour of every day of every year in America.

- If one wants to start a sexual relationship, he or she usually doesn't have to look far to find a willing partner (Proverbs 9:14–16).

Second, sin is progressive. It's a slide on a slippery slope that goes down, down, down. For years a cigarette company said, "Come on up to Marlboro Country"; but that's a lie. The road into the far country is always downhill. Jonah went down to Joppa, down into the ship (Jonah 1:3), down into the sea, down into the fish's mouth, and down to the sea bottom.

Think of sin's downward progression:

- Walking with the ungodly leads to standing with sinners; standing with sinners leads to sitting with the scornful (Psalm 1:1; Matthew 26:58, 69–75).
- Anger leads to violence; wrath leads to hatred; hatred leads to murder (Genesis 4:6, 8; Proverbs 27:3; Daniel 2:12; 1 John 3:15);
- Jealousy and envy lead to cruelty, slander, and vengeance (Proverbs 6:34; 27:4; Song of Solomon 8:6; Judges 19:29–30);
- Disobedience to parents leads to lying to parents (Romans 1:30; Ephesians 4:15; cf. Genesis 26:7; Colossians 3:9);
- One lie leads to more lies (cf. John 8:44);
- Covetousness leads to stealing and violence (Joshua 7:21; 1 Kings 21:1, 15; Micah 2:1–2; Mark 7:21–22; Ephesians 4:28; 2 Peter 2:3);
- R-rated movies lead to X-rated movies; soft-core porn leads to hard-core porn (Matthew 5:28; 1 Peter 2:11); pornography leads to sexual sins, often even rape and child molestation;
- Lust leads to fornication (Matthew 5:28; 1 Corinthians 6:18); dancing and petting lead to fornication (cf. Galatians 5:19–21).
- Perverted thoughts lead to homosexuality (Romans 1:26–27; cf. Genesis 19:5; Leviticus 18:22; Judges 19:22; 1 Corinthians 6:9; 1 Timothy 1:10; Jude 7, 10); homosexuality leads to pedophilia (child rape/molestation) (cf. 2 Timothy 3:13).
- Smoking cigarettes often precedes smoking marijuana (1 Corinthians 6:19–20); smoking marijuana usually leads to using harder drugs (Romans 6:13).

Third, a sinful life is a turbulent life. Jonah found himself in a storm. It usually does not take long for those who forsake Christ to find turmoil in their lives (Proverbs 4:19; 15:10; Jeremiah 2:19; Romans 6:21).

THE PRODIGAL SON'S FEET WERE
SWIFT IN RUNNING TO MISCHIEF (LUKE 15:11–17)

The prodigal son ran away from home. This young man is presented as a warning to us because each of us has run away from our Father (Romans 3:23; Ephesians 2:13–17). Let us try to picture him as he was. It is likely that

- He grew up in a wealthy, godly home.
- His father had been strict on him—as good parents are.
- He grew tired of rules, restrictions, and regulations.
- He reached the legal age of adulthood and wanted to make his own decisions.

So he demanded his inheritance money from his father. He wanted to move out and start living for himself. This desire is not necessarily evil (cf. Genesis 2:24)—his father might have even had good feelings about it—but the boy's intent seems to have been to experiment with sin; at the least, he made poor decisions.

The background to this makes an interesting study. Under Jewish law a firstborn son received a double portion of his father's property (Deuteronomy 21:16–17; cf. Psalm 16:5–6). Thus this younger son would have only received one-third of the father's possessions. It was not uncommon for a father to dispose of his possessions before he died (cf. Genesis 25:5–6), as took place in Jesus' story. According to the laws of the East, on becoming of age, a son could ask for his portion of the inheritance and unless there was some good reason why he should not receive it, he would receive it early.

Notice carefully the steps of the prodigal's downfall:

He desired the far country of sin. When the prodigal came to his father and made the request, perhaps his heart was already in the far country. When a person reaches the far country in his thinking, it is usually not long until he reaches it in his living. In the early morning of time, Adam and Eve desired independence (Genesis 3:1–10), and soon fulfilled it on the darkest day of their lives. Like King Manasseh (2 Chronicles 33:1–2), many today desire independence from God and His rules. The young desire to kick up their heels; adults become self-sufficient and self-serving; the aged become hardened in a life of sin. This desire for independence has caused all men to depart from God (Romans 3:23), and the majority to stay there (Matthew 7:13–14). Most people do not want anyone, even God, directing their lives (cf. Jeremiah 10:23). They seek to direct their lives and their religion by their own wisdom (Mark 7:7–9).

He made a demand of his father. Perhaps he did not at first intend to spend his money in riotous living, but only wanted to be free to make his own decisions. If so, this tender lamb became easy prey for the old lion (cf. 1 Peter 5:8). It is easy for a child of God to drift away from his spiritual home (Hebrews 2:1), especially when big changes take place in life: going to college, marriage, new job, new child, the empty nest, failing health.

He departed into the far country. He left his father (cf. 2 Timothy 4:10). He went into the far country by determined forethought. The prodigal son was not lost through his own carelessness, like the sheep in the earlier parable (Luke 15:4–7), or through the carelessness of others, like the coin in the second parable (Luke 15:8–10).

Some might be surprised that the father would allow the son to go to the far country. Since the father represents God, we see that all are free to serve Satan. All the soldiers in the Lord's army are volunteers. There are no conscripts in the army of Prince Immanuel. Man, as a free moral agent, is privileged to exercise his power of choice (Joshua 24:15).

This son wanted to enjoy the pleasures of sin for a season (cf. Hebrews 11:25). Although he may not have deliberately wanted to injure his father, nevertheless, he was willing to break his daddy's heart in order to have his own way. The desire for self-rule is at the very root of sin, and it is the downfall of many souls. It is the essence of sin. Many people deliberately forsake the Lord and go into the far country. They decide to eat, drink, and be merry regardless of the consequences. They determine to pursue self-rule instead God-rule. This journey into the far country represents the separation of spiritual death (Isaiah 59:1–2; James 2:26).

He digressed into riotous living. He became a spendthrift, a profligate, and a prodigal, which means "wasteful." He did not invest his inheritance, he wasted it (Proverbs 5:8–14; 6:26; 18:9; 21:17, 20; 23:19–22; 28:7; 29:3; Ecclesiastes 11:9–10; Romans 13:13–14; 1 Peter 4:3–4; 2 Peter 2:13). As long as people serve the devil, they are wasting their lives, money, influence, and eternal future.

The prodigal found himself in an evil environment and gave in to sin (cf. Psalm 1:1–2). It is likely that the evaluation given by the elder brother was an accurate one (Luke 15:30). He did what he wanted, when he wanted, for as long as he wanted, at least until the money ran out. If anyone ever could have enjoyed sinful pleasures—it should have been this boy. He was young, full of life, free from cares, without restrictions, rich, and eager for opportunities to sin. But he found Satan's promises are empty lies. We, too, have gone the way of our sins and ended up where we did not want to be (Romans

6:23; 1 Corinthians 6:9–11; Ephesians 2:2–3; 4:17–19; 5:11–12; Colossians 3:5–7; Titus 3:3).

He suffered destitution and degradation. The prodigal boy's itinerary listed "far country" and maybe under that, "beaches, bars, and brothels." But he had to read the very fine print to find "pig farm." His summer trip took him farther than he intended to go. Once we board sin's train, it can be awfully hard to disembark.

Not only was there a famine in the land, he experienced a severe, personal famine. He was destitute, moneyless, jobless, and friendless (cf. Psalm 73:27; Proverbs 27:8). In sin, there is a famine of those things upon which the soul subsists. A man in sin is in the wrong element. God made the fish for the water; he made the bird for the air. They cannot exchange places without dying (cf. Romans 6:19–21). God created man for righteousness—when man gets into sin the result is spiritual death (Romans 6:23; 2 Timothy 2:25–26).

Thankfully, the prodigal son was just as swift in running back to his father as he had been in running away from him. He came to himself, arose, and went back home to his father. This illustrates that we can come back home to God from whatever far country we have visited (cf. Luke 8:35; Psalm 73:20; Ecclesiastes 9:3; Acts 2:37; 16:29–30; 26:11–19; Ephesians 2:4–5; 5:14).

SATAN'S FEET WERE SWIFT IN RUNNING TO MISCHIEF

Satan ran swiftly to cause trouble for Job (Job 1:7). Given permission by God to destroy Job's wealth, Satan wasted no time. A sequence of disasters befell Job with lightning speed. Each disaster followed hard on the heels of the previous one. This was not the last time we see Satan eager to destroy man. He was also ready to "sift Peter as wheat" (Luke 22:31). He was on hand to tempt Jesus in the wilderness (Matthew 4:1–10), and left Him only "for a season" (Luke 4:13).

In contrast, the feet of Jesus often brought Him swiftly to where He could help and heal (cf. Acts 1:1). Back and forth He went—north and south, east and west—always seeking out the lost, the diseased, the downtrodden, and the distressed (Luke 8:35; 10:39; Acts 10:38). His feet were never in a hurry; they never got Him there too late or too early.

We should be very eager to avoid sin (Ecclesiastes 5:1; cf. Isaiah 59:7). In Proverbs, it is interesting to follow the warnings given to our feet. "Withdraw thy foot from thy neighbour's house; lest he be weary of thee, and so hate thee" (25:17). He warned again, "He that hasteth with his feet sinneth" (19:2). In the immediate context of Proverbs 6:18, which mentions swift feet, Solomon spoke of the wicked man who "speaketh with his feet" (6:13). Solomon warned of the adulterous woman: "Her feet go down to death; her steps take hold on hell" (5:5). "(She is loud and stubborn; her feet abide not in her house: Now is she without, now in the streets, and lieth in wait at every corner)" (7:11–12; cf. Genesis 18:9; 1 Timothy 5:13–14; Titus 2:5).

Several New Testament passages also admonish "foot care."

- "To give light to them that sit in darkness and in the shadow of death, to guide our feet into the way of peace" (Luke 1:79).

- "And how shall they preach, except they be sent? As it is written, How beautiful are the feet of them that preach the gospel of peace, and bring glad tidings of good things!" (Romans 10:15).

- "And your feet shod with the preparation of the gospel of peace" (Ephesians 6:15).

- "And make straight paths for your feet, lest that which is lame be turned out of the way; but let it rather be healed" (Hebrews 12:13).

The Bible makes a strong case for being deliberate in our actions, especially when we are making decisions in new areas (Proverbs 1:16; 14:29; 21:5; 25:8; 28:22; Job 31:5; Ecclesiastes 7:9; Isaiah 28:16). It counsels us to be "swift to hear" but "slow to speak, slow to wrath" (James 1:19).

At the same time, we are to run away quickly from evil. Joseph practiced this principle when he ran from Potiphar's wife (Genesis 39:12). Paul wrote, "Let love be without dissimulation. Abhor that which is evil; cleave to that which is good" (Romans 12:9; Psalm 34:14; 36:4; 45:7; 97:10; 101:3; 119:104, 163; Proverbs 8:13; Amos 5:15; Hebrews 1:9).

Let us consider well the examples of Jonah, the prodigal son, and Satan, and where their feet led them. Where are my feet leading me?

Questions to Consider and Discuss

1. Have you found the statement, sin lies "at the door"—nearby—(Genesis 4:7) to be true in your life?

2. Which of these statements would you like to discuss further?
    a. The road into the "far country" is always downhill.
    b. When a person reaches the far country in his thinking, it is not long until he reaches it in his living.
    c. All the soldiers in the Lord's army are volunteers.
    d. Once we board sin's train, it can be awfully hard to disembark.
    e. "Withdraw thy foot from thy neighbour's house; lest he be weary of thee, and so hate thee" (Proverbs 25:17).
    f. "Her feet go down to death; her steps take hold on hell . . . (She is loud and stubborn; her feet abide not in her house: now is she without, now in the streets, and lieth in wait at every corner)" (Proverbs 5:5; 7:11–12).

3. Give some examples from the Bible and from recent news events showing how "one sin leads to another."

4. What advice do you think young people need before leaving for college or going out into the world for the first time?

5. What are the steps to return to God from the "far country"?

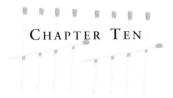

CHAPTER TEN

A FALSE WITNESS
THAT SPEAKETH LIES

Proverbs 6:19

The angler caught a fish so big he dislocated both shoulders describing it." We smile and wink at some of the dishonesty that goes on around us, and we frown and fret at other times. God certainly takes notice. Forms of lying accounted for 28.5 percent—two out of seven—of the things He hates in Solomon's famous list.

Solomon stated a profound truth by saying, "A faithful witness will not lie: but a false witness will utter lies" (Proverbs 14:5). No matter the circumstances, no matter the stakes, no matter the political correctness, no matter the financial cost or gain, a faithful person always tells the truth. A false witness will bow to pressures and prejudices and utter a lie. We should always strive to be like Jesus who is "the faithful witness" (Revelation 1:5).

In Proverbs, the wise man repeatedly condemns the sin of false witness (Proverbs 6:19; 12:17; 14:5, 25; 19:5, 9, 28; 21:28; 24:28). The word *speaketh* in "a false[1] witness that speaketh lies"[2] is an expressive word. It literally means to "blow out" or "breathe out" lies[3] (cf. Psalm 10:5, "He puffeth at them").

God considered being a false witness serious enough to include a warning against it in His ten basic rules for life—it is the ninth of the *Ten Commandments* (Exodus

20:16; Deuteronomy 5:20). Jesus included it when asked by the rich young ruler which commandments he was to keep. Jesus said, "Thou shalt do no murder, Thou shalt not commit adultery, Thou shalt not steal, Thou shalt not bear false witness, Honour thy father and thy mother: and, Thou shalt love thy neighbour as thyself" (Matthew 19:16–19). Bearing false witness is one of the sins that comes out of an evil heart (Matthew 15:19). Paul included it again in his discussion of the law of love (Romans 13:9).

In his *Commentary on Exodus*, Matthew Henry observed, "Thou shalt not bear false witness" forbids three things:

- Speaking falsely in any matter, lying, equivocating, and any way devising and designing to deceive our neighbor.
- Speaking unjustly against our neighbor, to the prejudice of his reputation; and,
- Bearing false witness against him, laying to his charge things that he knows not, either judicially, upon oath (by which the third commandment, and the sixth and eighth, as well as this, may be broken), or extra-judicially, in common converse. This third naturally involves the guilt of both the first two.

Let us look at these in reverse order—from specific to general—legal false witness, social false witness, and general false witness.

LEGAL FALSE WITNESS

False witnesses, dishonest prosecutors and lawyers, and perjurious experts make our headlines far more often than they should. Take, for example, the case of Kenneth Peasley who prosecuted two men accused in a 1992 triple-slaying at a market in Tucson. In a highly unusual decision, the Arizona Supreme Court upheld a recommendation for disbarment of the state's most "successful" capital homicide prosecutor, for suborning and exploiting known perjury.

The use of false testimony in the trial "could not have been more harmful to the justice system," wrote Justice Michael D. Ryan for the unanimous court. "A prosecutor who deliberately presents false testimony, especially in a capital case, has caused incalculable injury to the integrity of the legal profession and the justice system."

Peasley was admitted to the state bar in 1974 and conducted about 250 felony cases, 140 of which were homicides, the court said. Sixty of the cases were capital murder trials. In a ruling overturning the conviction of one of the defendants in 2002, the Supreme

Court said Peasley intentionally deceived the jury to paper over weaknesses in his case. Some of the people he convicted were executed.[4]

THE LAW'S REQUIREMENTS

Our courts require "the truth, the whole truth, and nothing but the truth." Ancient Jewish courts were based upon the maxim, "Thou shalt not bear false witness against thy neighbour" (Exodus 20:16). This command is repeated in the same form in English in Deuteronomy 5:20. Although the English form is in both cases false "witness," the Hebrew word is different. In the Exodus passage, the meaning is "lying or untrue"; in Deuteronomy the meaning is "insincere, empty, frivolous." Barclay notes that the meaning is not essentially different, but it might be said that Exodus emphasizes the nature of the evidence and Deuteronomy the spirit in which evidence is given.

An interesting fact about Jewish law is that the man who refused to give evidence when it would have helped the court reach a fair verdict was condemned as severely as the man who gave false testimony (Leviticus 5:1). The sin of deadly silence was as real as the sin of false speech.

Under the Jewish system, no man was to be condemned on uncorroborated evidence. The law stated in three different places that the evidence of one witness was never enough for a guilty verdict. In two cases this principle relates to crimes involving the death penalty (Numbers 35:30; Deuteronomy 17:6). In the third case it is extended to cover any crime (Deuteronomy 19:15). The New Testament often refers to this requirement of two or three witnesses (Matthew 18:16; 2 Corinthians 13:1; 1 Timothy 5:19; Hebrews 10:28).

There were two rules that would make a person hesitant to bear false witness:

- In a capital case when the penalty was stoning to death and the defendant was convicted, then the leading witness for the prosecution had to push him down a precipice and roll the first great stone upon him (Sanhedrin 5.4; cf. Luke 4:29; Acts 7:58–59).

- In a case in which one was suspected of making a false accusation in court, God gave the procedure for dealing with it (Deuteronomy 19:15–20). The judges were to make "diligent inquisition" (19:18). If a person was found to have offered false testimony, then he was to receive the punishment that he tried to get for his brother (19:19). The false witness, says the Mishnah, shall pay the whole penalty (Baba Kamma 7.3). If this punishment is impossible, as, for instance, when a witness gave false evidence as to a child's legitimacy, then the false witness was given forty stripes; if the penalty itself was forty stripes, the false witness was given eighty stripes (Makkoth 1.1, 3).[5]

Such strict procedures would obviously benefit the innocent person, but God also gave two social reasons for this punishment:

- It would "put the evil away from among you" (Deuteronomy 19:19). This person would learn a hard lesson and would be unlikely to commit the same crime in the future. In the case of capital crimes, he would obviously commit no more evil after his execution.

- It would serve as a deterrent to sin: "And those which remain shall hear, and fear, and shall henceforth commit no more any such evil among you" (Deuteronomy 19:20).

THE JEWS' PRACTICE

William Barclay included research from the Mishnah that gives more details about the strict regulations Jewish courts followed:[6]

- The two witnesses were to be examined independently, and hearsay evidence was absolutely excluded. A man could only testify to that which he had actually heard or seen (Sanhedrin 3:6).

- Any contradiction between the witnesses rendered the whole evidence invalid (Sanhedrin 5:2).

- In a case involving the death penalty, the witness was to be solemnly warned that he was responsible for the life of the man on trial and for that of his unborn posterity (Sanhedrin 4.5). A man was considered a better judge if he rigorously cross-questioned witnesses and tested evidence (Sanhedrin 5.2).

- Any man who was under suspicion himself could neither give evidence nor judgment in a case (Bekhoroth 7.3). If any witness took payment for his evidence, or any judge for his sitting in judgment, then the testimony and the verdict were both invalid (Bekhoroth 4.6).

- No relation of the man on trial was eligible to give evidence, and the disqualifying relationships were carefully listed—kinsmen, father, brother, father's brother, mother's brother, sister's husband, father's sister's husband, mother's sister's husband, mother's husband, father-in-law, wife's sister's husband, together with all their sons and sons-in-law. A stepson may not give evidence, but his sons could. In general, no one qualified to be the heir of the person on trial can give evidence (Sanhedrin 3.3, 4; Makkoth 1.8). Neither a friend nor an enemy could give evidence. The friend was described as one who had been the accused's groomsman, and an enemy as one who had not spoken to him for three days because of the difference (Sanhedrin 3.5).

- People following certain trades and professions were barred—a dice-player, a usurer, a pigeon-flyer, a slave, a trafficker in the seventh year produce[7] (Rosh Hashanah 1.8; Sanhedrin 3.3).

BIBLE EXAMPLES OF FALSE WITNESSES

Satan used false witnesses to secure the death of Christ. His enemies knew they could get nothing on Jesus. Any honest witness would tell of His feeding the five thousand with a little lad's lunch, of His ridding the Gadarene demoniac of a legion of evil spirits, of His healing sick and injured people, and of His raising the dead—Jairus's daughter, the son of the widow of Nain, and Lazarus. Blind Bartimaeus would tell how he received his sight, Zaccheus of being accepted, the woman at the well of being made pure. Malchus would soon be able to show the ear that had been replaced, and others could show limbs that were restored (Matthew 15:30–31).

These religious leaders were not interested in honest witnesses, though. They wanted false witnesses who would distort Jesus' words, take them out of context, and make them mean something Jesus didn't say. Matthew records,

> Now the chief priests, and elders, and all the council, sought false witness against Jesus, to put him to death; but found none: yea, though many false witnesses came, yet found they none. At the last came two false witnesses, And said, This fellow said, I am able to destroy the temple of God, and to build it in three days (Matthew 26:59–61).

Note that Matthew 26:60 says, "Many false witnesses came." Mark adds, "For many bare false witness against him, but their witness agreed not together . . . But neither so did their witness agree together" (Mark 14:56–59). Liars are never in short supply. According to the Law of Moses, these should have received the punishment they were trying to get for Jesus.

False witnesses appeared at the trial of Stephen (Acts 6:13).

Stephen faced false witnesses:

> Then there arose certain of the synagogue, which is called the synagogue of the
> Libertines, and Cyrenians, and Alexandrians, and of them of Cilicia and of Asia,
> disputing with Stephen . . . And set up false witnesses, which said, This man
> ceaseth not to speak blasphemous words against this holy place, and the law: for
> we have heard him say, that this Jesus of Nazareth shall destroy this place, and shall
> change the customs which Moses delivered us (Acts 6:9–14).

SOCIAL FALSE WITNESS

Matthew Henry's second application of "Thou shalt not bear false witness" was "speaking unjustly against our neighbor, to the prejudice of his reputation." This is more
general than a legal courtroom testimony. It includes slandering a person's name under
any circumstance.

What metaphor would serve to explain the work of a false witness? The Holy Spirit
chose terms related to physical violence and war. He said, "A man that beareth false witness against his neighbour is a maul, and a sword, and a sharp arrow" (Proverbs 25:18).
A more modern writer used the same figure: "'Tis slander, whose edge is sharper than
the sword." Perhaps if you have been a victim, you have come to disagree with the
child's rhyme: "Sticks and stones may break my bones, but words will never hurt me."

David was falsely accused, and it almost destroyed him. He prayed,

> Deliver me not over unto the will of mine enemies: for false witnesses are risen up
> against me, and such as breathe out cruelty. I had fainted, unless I had believed to
> see the goodness of the LORD in the land of the living. Wait on the LORD: be of
> good courage, and he shall strengthen thine heart: wait, I say, on the LORD (Psalm
> 27:12–14; cf. 35:11–15).

Note that David dealt with false testimony by:

- Maintaining his integrity—he did not fight fire with fire. It is better to be
  lied about than to lie.
- Prayer—he spoke honestly to God, in contrast to those who spoke dis-
  honestly about him.
- Believing in the goodness of God—he chose to focus on God's character
  rather than man's cruelty.
- Patience—he waited for the Lord to correct it.

GENERAL FALSE WITNESS

The matter of the false witness must be seen against the background of falsehood in general.[8] Matthew Henry's statement, "Speaking falsely in any matter, lying, equivocating, and any way devising and designing to deceive our neighbor," suggests a general application. Bearing false witness can occur outside of a formal court and does not refer only to direct slander. False witness is a kind of lie. The many condemnations of lying in the Old Testament show the prevalence of it and God's disdain for it (Hosea 10:13; Isaiah 59:3–4; Jeremiah 9:3).

Frequent threats and warnings are given to those who practice falsehood and lying (Isaiah 28:17; Psalm 63:11; 101:7). Everyone who loves or practices falsehood will be shut out of heaven (Revelation 21:27; 22:15). Nowhere is condemnation more fierce than for a prophet who speaks and teaches with "lying divinations" (Ezekiel 13:9; 21:29; 22:28; Isaiah 9:15; Jeremiah 14:14; 23:25–26, 32; 27:10, 14, 16, 18; Zechariah 10:2).

On the other hand, commendations are given for truth-telling. The wise man prayed: "Remove far from me falsehood and lying" (Proverbs 30:8). Zephaniah pictured a time when "the remnant of Israel shall not do iniquity, nor speak lies; neither shall a deceitful tongue be found in their mouth (Zephaniah 3:13).

It is interesting to see from where lies come. What makes people tell lies?[9]

- **Some lie out of habit.** Lying often starts early in life and can become ingrained—what we call "second nature" (Psalm 58:3; 62:4; Isaiah 28:15). Many young people start out telling lies and never stop. George Washington gained no popularity among such youths by the retelling of that old "cherry tree" story!

- **Some lie out of malice.** The Bible often speaks of the whisperer in unflattering terms (e.g., Proverbs 16:28). Paul said that this sin of whispering malicious gossip was one of the sins of the contemporary world to which he preached (Romans 1:28–29). It was also one of the sins that troubled the church at Corinth (2 Corinthians 12:20). William Barclay pointed out three closely connected New Testament Greek words. The word *diabolos*,[10] meaning "a slanderer," is one thing women are forbidden to be (1 Timothy 3:11). *Blasphemia*, when used of men, means "insulting slander." It is one of the forbidden sins in Paul's list to the Ephesians (4:31). A third word is *katalalia*, which the King James Version translates "backbiting" and "evil-speaking"

(2 Corinthians 12:20; 1 Peter 2:1). Anyone who enjoys gossip, who repeats gossip, and who initiates gossip would be shocked to be called a malicious liar, but that is precisely what he or she is.

- **Some lie out of fear.** Perhaps the first of all lies in a person's life, and continuing to the end of life, is a lie told out of fear. Epicurus was not a religious man; he did not believe in "the gods" at all, and he believed that religion was a delusion. But from the practical, political point of view, he always believed that truth must be told, for once a man tells an untruth there is always at the back of his mind the nagging fear that he will be found out—and there is no happiness in that lifestyle.

- **Some lie out of carelessness.** When one is too lazy or busy to ascertain facts before repeating something, he may lie carelessly. What we only listen to with one ear, we should not repeat with both lips.

- **Some lie to boast.** Young people tend to make themselves out worse than they are. They want to appear rebellious, edgy, or experienced in sin. Many adults want to appear better than they are.

- **Some lie for profit.** Advertising and business deals are not always what they seem to be in the print ads or in the salesman's pitch.

- **Some lie for propaganda purposes.** In war, "truth is the first casualty." This might also be said of high-stakes political campaigns. If we could magically treat our newspapers as dictator-led nations do theirs and erase all the lies told about the opposite side, how many blank columns there might be! We do well to remember the African Proverb that states, "Who lies for you will lie against you."

It is possible to tell lies without saying a word, or even when speaking the truth! How? Silence can leave an untrue impression. How? (1) By neglecting to defend a slandered character, silence implies consent. (2) A shrug of the shoulders, a compression of the lips, a motion of the hand, a nod, or a lifting of the eyebrows may be more than enough to ruin a reputation or a soul. A half-truth can be a whole lie. There may be some basis of truth in what is told, but if a significant detail or circumstance is left out, then it becomes a lie by leaving a false impression.

Each of the ten commandments protects something of value—the home, marriage, property rights. The ninth commandment protects good names—our own and our neighbor's. We are all mirrors in which our neighbors' characters are in some way reflected. Therefore, we must be very careful with the reputation of others. The Bible states the value of a good name—reputation: "A good name is better than precious ointment" (Ecclesiastes 7:1); "A good name is rather to be chosen than great riches" (Proverbs 22:1).[11] While silver and gold are the most valuable substances in the world to many people, Christians realize some things are more valuable than these things that are so temporary in light of eternity (2 Peter 3:10–11; Matthew 6:19–20).

The reputation of our neighbor, whether he be a company president or a common laborer, ought to be as precious to us as our own. Human laws try to limit theft and murder by punishment, but they usually do not punish for thefts and murders committed by the tongue. We recognize the sinful power of the human hand but may forget the power of evil in the human tongue. Tongues can steal; lips can murder. The mouth can kill a neighbor's reputation and rob one of that which makes him poor indeed, and does not enrich the thief (to paraphrase Shakespeare).

A good name is one of the most valuable assets we have. A man's name represents all that he is and has been since he entered the world. It will either remind those who know him of honesty and integrity or of dishonesty and corruptness. Thus, when a man loses his good name, he has lost something that money cannot replace. This is the reason we spend so much time reminding young people to carefully guard their reputations. We instruct them to choose carefully their associates, because if their companions do not have a good name, then their names will also lose luster (1 Corinthians 15:33). Whether young or old, we must make sure that we carefully guard our good names.

It may be extremely difficult—if not impossible—for a person to clear away all the dirt which has been thrown on him by a single liar. Many a man's reputation has been darkened all his life by the malicious tales of an enemy. The philosophers and poets have often touched on this theme:

- Joseph Hall said, "A reputation once broken may possibly be repaired, but the world will always keep their eyes on the spot where the crack was."

- Ben Franklin stated, "Glass, china, and reputation are easily cracked and never well mended."

- Anwar-I-Suheli said, "The broken string may be joined, but a knot will always remain."

- An Italian proverb stated, "Who has a bad name is half hanged."

- Mark Twain observed, "One of the striking differences between a cat and a lie is that a cat has only nine lives."

- Ed Howe pointed out, "What people say behind your back *is* your standing in the community."

The Bible rarely repeats itself, but God reiterated this truth: "A false witness shall not be unpunished, and he that speaketh lies shall not escape." "A false witness shall not be unpunished, and he that speaketh lies shall perish." "A false witness shall perish" (Proverbs 19:5, 9; 21:28). God's vengeance, says the prophet, is against those who swear falsely (Malachi 3:5). To avoid this heavy condemnation we must seek to be like Him who is the truth (John 14:6).

Questions to Consider and Discuss

1. What two rules made a person hesitant to bear false witness under the Old Testament law?

2. From your experiences, which statements strike you as true?
   a. 'Tis slander, whose edge is sharper than the sword.
   b. What we only listen to with one ear, we should not repeat with both lips.
   c. Who lies for you will lie against you (African proverb).
   d. "A good name is rather to be chosen than great riches" (Proverbs 22:1).
   e. A reputation once broken may possibly be repaired, but the world will always keep their eyes on the spot where the crack was.
   f. Glass, china, and reputation are easily cracked and never well mended (Ben Franklin)
   g. Who has a bad name is half hanged (Italian proverb).
   h. One of the striking differences between a cat and a lie is that a cat has only nine lives (Mark Twain).
   i. What people say behind your back *is* your standing in the community (Ed Howe).

3. Under Jewish law, the man who refused to give evidence when it would have helped the court reach a fair verdict was condemned as severely as what man? (Leviticus 5:1).

4. Why do you think God emphasized the need to "put the evil away from among you" so often in the Old Testament? (Deuteronomy 19:19).

5. Which of these do you think best describes the wounds inflicted by a false witness: a maul, and a sword, and a sharp arrow? (Proverbs 25:18).

6. How did David deal with false witnesses? (Psalm 27:12–14; 35:11–15).

7. What are some of the reasons that people tell lies?

CHAPTER ELEVEN

HE THAT SOWETH DISCORD AMONG BRETHREN

Proverbs 6:19

A new student was brought into a Vacation Bible School class about an hour before dismissal. The little boy was missing an arm, and since the class was in progress, the teacher had no opportunity to learn the cause or his state of adjustment. She was afraid that one of the children would comment on his handicap and embarrass him. There was no opportunity to caution them, so she proceeded as carefully as possible. As class came to a close, she began to relax.

She asked the class to join her in their usual closing ceremony. "Let's make our churches," she said. "Here's the church and here's the steeple, open the doors and there's . . . " The awful truth of her own actions struck her. The very thing she had feared that the children would do, she had done. As she stood there speechless, the little girl sitting next to the boy reached over with her left hand and placed it up to his right hand and said, "Davey, let's make the church together."[1]

This story may be seen as a parable of our search for oneness in Christ: to put our inadequate, handicapped lives alongside the lives of others and to pray, "Let's make the church together." Let's examine each part of the warning: "He that soweth discord among brethren."

"HE THAT SOWETH . . . "

The last entry on God's list of seven hated things takes the form of a farming analogy. Solomon says that God hates him "that soweth discord among brethren." The Bible says much about sowing. The word *sow* (including *sowed, sown, sowing, soweth*) is used eighty times in Scripture. Many of these are literal references to farming—broadcasting seed in a field for cultivation. Others refer metaphorically to the acts of one's life. For instance, Paul wrote, "Be not deceived; God is not mocked: for whatsoever a man soweth, that shall he also reap. For he that soweth to his flesh shall of the flesh reap corruption; but he that soweth to the Spirit shall of the Spirit reap life everlasting" (Galatians 6:7–8). The righteous sow the positive seeds of

- God's Word (Psalm 126:5–6; Mark 4:14; John 4:36–37).
- Righteousness (Proverbs 11:18; Hosea 10:12).
- Spiritual things (1 Corinthians 9:11).
- Financial giving (2 Corinthians 9:6, 10).
- Peace—the seed of righteousness produces peace (James 3:18).

Jesus is the healer of broken homes, the reconciler of estranged brethren, the Prince of Peace. He matched Peter the doer with John the dreamer; Simon the Zealot with Matthew the publican; down-to-earth Philip with guileless Nathanael.

Sinners are also sowers, but they sow seeds that have negative results. Hosea speaks of those who "have sown the wind, and they shall reap the whirlwind" (Hosea 8:7). Negative seeds may include:

- Wickedness (Job 4:8).
- Strife (Proverbs 16:28). Satan the meddler stirred up Cain against Abel, Ishmael against Isaac, Esau against Jacob, and the sons of Jacob against Joseph.
- Iniquity (Proverbs 22:8).
- An idol's name (Nahum 1:14).
- Discord (Proverbs 6:14, 19).

"DISCORD . . . "

The word *discord* is only used twice in the entire Bible, and both instances are in Proverbs. "A naughty person, a wicked man, walketh with a froward mouth. He winketh with his eyes, he speaketh with his feet, he teacheth with his fingers; frowardness

is in his heart, he deviseth mischief continually; he soweth discord" (6:12–14).[2]
Proverbs 6:19 says, "A false witness that speaketh lies, and he that soweth discord among
brethren." The word used here comes from a root (*madown*) that means "a contest or
quarrel; brawling, contention."

Have you ever heard of someone who had a falling out? Have you wondered what that
meant, or what the origin of that phrase was? It seems to date all the way back to
Genesis. Joseph "sent his brethren away, and they departed: and he said unto them,
See that ye fall not out by the way" (Genesis 45:24). He knew his brothers were apt to
quarrel. He had forgiven them for their mistreatment of him years before and had been
united with them, so he urged them not to let a quarrel divide them. The Lord Jesus
commanded us to love one another; whatever happens, or has happened, we must "fall
not out." For we are brethren, we have all one Father (Malachi 2:10); we all serve the
same King.

WHAT ARE THE SEEDS OF DISCORD?

James asked: "From whence come wars and fightings among you?" (James 4:1). Where
do divisions originate?

Divisions come where there is a lack of love. Solomon traced discord to its genesis:
"Hatred stirreth up strifes: but love covereth all sins" (Proverbs 10:12). By contrast, Paul
explained that "charity suffereth long" (1 Corinthians 13:4). James and Peter echo the
truth that "love covers a multitude of sins" in the new covenant (James 5:20; 1 Peter 4:8).

According to one legend, two shopkeepers were bitter rivals. Their stores were directly
across the street from each other, so they spent each day keeping track of each other's
business. If one got a customer, he would smile in triumph at his rival. One night an
angel appeared to one shopkeeper in a dream and said, "I will give you anything you
ask, but whatever you receive, your competitor will receive twice as much. Would you
be rich? You can be very rich, but he will be twice as wealthy. Do you wish to live a
long and healthy life? You can, but his life will be longer and healthier. What is your
desire?" The man frowned, thought for a while, and then said, "Here is my request:
Strike me blind in one eye!"

A person with a jealous, unloving heart finds it easier to show sympathy and "weep with
those who weep" than to exhibit joy and "rejoice with those who rejoice"[3] (Romans
12:15). Love considers the danger that words may pose to their hearer—they can be

poison (James 3:8) or burn someone (James 3:6). We should use them cautiously, realizing that we could become a stumbling block to a new or weak Christian (cf. Matthew 18:6).

One little girl about eight-years-old loved to travel with her father, a watch repairman. On one trip, she looked up and asked him, "Daddy, where do babies come from?" He sat without answering for quite some time. They just listened to the clatter of the train rolling down the track. Soon, the train pulled into the depot. He asked the girl to carry his large tool case. She reached for the handle and pulled with all her might. She struggled but could not lift it. Then she looked at her father and said, "Daddy, it's too heavy for me."

He lifted it with ease and said, "I'll carry it for you." As they walked along, he told her, "When you tried to lift the case you realized that it was too great a burden for you to lift right now. You need to gain some physical maturity. I've chosen not to answer your question because it would be too heavy a burden at your young age. When you mature emotionally, you'll be more able to bear the answer."

She had come to appreciate the wise love her father had for her innocent youth. May we be as considerate of others who may not be able to easily bear criticism. Love would rather suffer wrong than do wrong (1 Corinthians 6:7).

Divisions come where there are idlers and busybodies. Paul wrote,

> But the younger widows refuse: for when they have begun to wax wanton against Christ, they will marry; having damnation, because they have cast off their first faith. And withal they learn to be idle, wandering about from house to house; and not only idle, but tattlers also and busybodies, speaking things which they ought not. I will therefore that the younger women marry, bear children, guide the house, give none occasion to the adversary to speak reproachfully. For some are already turned aside after Satan (1 Timothy 5:11–15).

Those busy sowing the seed of the kingdom do not have time and interest to sow seeds of discord. Those who eat the bread of idleness are often those who give the body— the church—indigestible attitudes. Both Peter and Paul warned of busybodies hindering Christianity (1 Peter 4:15; 2 Thessalonians 3:11).

However, each apostle uses a different word. "Busybody" (*allotriepiskopos*) in 1 Peter 4:15 means "overseeing others' affairs; an inspector; meddling with other people's concerns." In 2 Thessalonians 3:11"busybody" (*periergazomai*) means "to work all around, bustle about (meddle)." Put together, they show that God wants us to mind our business (Genesis 39:11; Proverbs 22:29; 1 Thessalonians 4:11), and His business (cf. Luke 2:49; Acts 6:3; Romans 12:11; 16:2), but we should not try to run other people's business for them. Let them "bear their own burden" (Galatians 6:5).

Divisions come where there is a lack of anger-control or a perverse enjoyment of strife (Proverbs 15:18; 29:22; 30:33; 1 Timothy 1:4; 4:7; 6:4, 5; 2 Timothy 2:14, 16, 23; Titus 3:9). Self-control is vital to ongoing personal relationships. Uncontrolled words, bursts of anger, and fits of rage lead to division. The division may last a thousand times longer than the anger. Some people just "love a good argument"—the adrenaline, the verbal swordplay, the chance to exercise quick wit, the "getting the last word in"—but not God's people. Christians have an aversion to strife for the sake of strife. They will endure it for a principle of truth, but they prefer to see the truth advanced in favor with all the people (Acts 2:46–47).

Divisions come where there is ungodliness. "An ungodly man diggeth up evil: and in his lips there is as a burning fire" (Proverbs 16:27). Since God is the "God of peace" (Romans 15:33; 16:20), and "is not the author of confusion, but of peace" (1 Corinthians 14:33), it follows that to be divisive is to be unlike God. God is "preaching peace by Jesus Christ" (Acts 10:36); sowers of discord are preaching a different gospel. God's common greeting[4] and constant desire for His people is: "Grace to you and peace from God our Father, and the Lord Jesus Christ" (Romans 1:7; cf. 1 Corinthians 1:3); to bring another greeting or to part with a different desire is to imitate someone other than God.

Divisions come where there is envy (James 3:14–16; cf. Genesis 26:14; 30:1–2; 37:11; Proverbs 6:34; 27:4; Song of Solomon 8:6; Matthew 27:18; Acts 7:9; 13:45; 17:5; Romans 1:29; 13:13; 1 Corinthians 3:3; 2 Corinthians 12:20; Galatians 5:15, 21, 26; Philippians 1:15; James 4:5–6; 1 John 3:12). Someone observed, "Envy is the only marksman that shoots at others and wounds herself." Shakespeare called it "the green sickness." Ruth Walsh defined it as "the art of counting another's blessings instead of one's own!" Antisthenes[5] said, "As rust corrupts iron, so envy corrupts man." A person who envies another's looks, position, finances, or family finds it easy to put a bad construction on their actions, words, or set of circumstances. Of course, "love envieth not" (1 Corinthians 13:4).

Divisions come where there is selfishness and lust for power, prestige, and control. James answered his question: "From whence come wars and fightings among you?" with, "Come they not hence, even of your lusts that war in your members?" (James 4:1). By contrast, in his dealings with Lot, Abraham exemplified the self-sacrificing attitude that God blesses: "Let there be not strife, I pray thee, between me and thee . . . for we be brethren" (Genesis 13:8). The rest of that story is well known: Lot lost everything in the fire that burned Sodom; Abraham maintained his status as a powerful, wealthy, and spiritual man of God.

Divisions come where there is pride and a desire for preeminence (Proverbs 28:25; Philippians 2:3). John said,

> I wrote unto the church: but Diotrephes, who loveth to have the preeminence among them, receiveth us not. Wherefore, if I come, I will remember his deeds which he doeth, prating against us with malicious words: and not content therewith, neither doth he himself receive the brethren, and forbiddeth them that would, and casteth them out of the church. Beloved, follow not that which is evil, but that which is good. He that doeth good is of God: but he that doeth evil hath not seen God (3 John 1:9–11).

The phrase "who loveth" (*ho philoproteuon*) is interesting. It literally means "who loveth the presidency." Diotrephes was most probably an officer in the church, likely an elder, but instead of letting the humility of Christ be his example (Philippians 2:3–5), he magnified himself and shamed Christ (cf. Luke 22:24–27; Romans 12:10; Titus 1:7–16).

HOW ARE THE SEEDS OF DISCORD SCATTERED?

Discord is scattered by preaching false doctrine (1 Kings 18:17–18; Acts 15:1–5, 24; 24:13; Romans 16:17–18; Galatians 1:7–9; 2:4; Philippians 3:2–3; Colossians 2:8; 2 Peter 2:1–2; 2 John 1:7–10; Jude 1:19). Truth unites; error unties. Note that the only difference in those two words is where the "t" is. That "t" stands for truth. God's Word is truth (John 17:17).

Discord is scattered by whispering. "A froward man soweth strife: and a whisperer separateth chief friends" (Proverbs 16:28; cf. 17:9; Genesis 3:1–13; 1 Samuel 24:9; Romans 1:29; 2 Corinthians 12:20).

Discord is scattered by a scornful, mocking attitude. Solomon said, "Cast out the scorner, and contention shall go out; yea, strife and reproach shall cease" (Proverbs 22:10; Genesis 21:9–10; Nehemiah 4:1–3).

Discord is scattered by gossiping. "Where no wood is, there the fire goeth out: so where there is no talebearer,[6] the strife ceaseth. As coals are to burning coals, and wood to fire; so is a contentious man to kindle strife" (Proverbs 26:20–21; 26:22; James 3:6).

"AMONG BRETHREN . . . "

The words *brother* and *brethren* are used 864 times in Scripture. There is a common brotherhood of man (cf. Acts 9:17), but a far more special brotherhood of the saved. Abraham's chief reason for avoiding strife with Lot was, "We be brethren" (Genesis 13:8). Earlier, when Moses tried to break up a fight between two Hebrews in Egypt, he used the same reasoning: "And the next day he showed himself unto them as they strove, and would have set them at one again, saying, Sirs, ye are brethren; why do ye wrong one to another?" (Acts 7:26; cf. Exodus 2:13–14).

Brotherly love is one of the most emphasized doctrines in the New Covenant. Paul wrote, "But as touching brotherly love ye need not that I write unto you: for ye yourselves are taught of God to love one another" (1 Thessalonians 4:9). The Holy Spirit commanded: "Let brotherly love continue" (Hebrews 13:1). Peter qualified the love as "fervent"[7] (1 Peter 1:22). He went so far as to say it was the above-all-things doctrine of his book: "And above all things have fervent charity among yourselves: for charity shall cover the multitude of sins" (1 Peter 4:8; cf. 2:17; 3:8). This is the equivalent of saying, "If you don't remember anything else that I said, don't forget this." The apostle of love goes one step further and says we ought to be willing to "to lay down our lives for the brethren" (1 John 3:16).

HOW SHOULD WE HANDLE OTHERS
WHO SOW DISCORD?

We should speak sensibly to them (2 Samuel 2:26–27). We should encourage others to see the harm in sowing discord so they will cease from it. Many good people get caught up in a sin, but when encouraged to forsake it, they willingly do so. A little thought and tact can often help defuse a volatile situation.

Once there were two people who had adjoining farms. One raised wheat and had children and large dogs. The other raised sheep. The sheep farmer was in a quandary because the dogs next door ran into his pastures and frightened his sheep. He spoke to his neighbor, but the raids continued. He thought about taking the neighbor to court. He even thought about poisoning the dogs. Then one day he found a better solution. Some new lambs were born and the sheep farmer gave each of his neighbor's children a lamb as a pet. They were delighted! Because of the pet lambs, the father could no longer let the dogs run around loose. He restrained them and taught them to leave the lambs and the sheep alone.[8] A peaceful solution is often available when we look for it.

We should refuse to let little things become major. Paul wrote, "But if thy brother be grieved with thy meat, now walkest thou not charitably. Destroy not him with thy meat, for whom Christ died. Let not then your good be evil spoken of" (Romans 14:15–16). Christians should not emphasize eating meat and observing days—little things, in the context of Romans 14—for these are not essential to religion. It will not be asked at the great day, "Who ate flesh, and who ate vegetables?" "Who kept days, and who did not?"[9] It will be asked, "Who feared God and worked righteousness, and who did not?" We should spend our zeal in the pursuit of the things that matter. We should ask ourselves, "Is this really important? Will it matter a year from now? Will God bring this up at the Judgment Day? Is it worth severing fellowship or a friendship?"

Consider the heart of the matter: "For the kingdom of God is not meat and drink; but righteousness, and peace, and joy in the Holy Ghost" (Romans 14:17). Righteousness, peace, and joy are comprehensive words. They summarize Christianity. As to God, our great concern is righteousness. As to ourselves, our great concern is joy. As to our brethren, our great concern is peace—to live in peace and love with them, following peace with all men. Note that one of the big three things of Christian living is peace. Often we can let little things disrupt the precious fellowship in Christ's church. We need to learn to get over things quickly. In this way, a little child might lead us (cf. Isaiah 11:6).

One little boy had a fight with his friend and said to his mother, "Mom, make Johnny go home." So she did.

The next day she noticed that they were playing again like nothing had happened. She said, "I thought that you were mad at each other."

"No," said her son. "Me and Johnny is good forgetters." He might not have known proper English, but he knew something that was more important.

We should love and pray for them. A third grader prayed a cute and incisive prayer, "Thank you for the people I like and those I don't like!" She may have been young, but she already knew there were problem people—those who are unlovely, obnoxious, rude, hard to get along with, and demoralizing. Job 14:1 says, "Man that is born of woman is of few days and full of troubles."

The apostle John had Diotrephes. You may run across someone like that. Jesus wants us to love such people and pray for them. In His most famous sermon, He included these memorable lines:

> Ye have heard that it hath been said, Thou shalt love thy neighbour, and hate thine enemy. But I say unto you, Love your enemies, bless them that curse you, do good to them that hate you, and pray for them which despitefully use you, and perse- cute you; that ye may be the children of your Father which is in heaven (Matthew 5:43–45).

Such praying might make a difference in them; it will certainly make a difference in us.

If they persist in sowing discord, we should mark and avoid them (Nehemiah 13:28; Psalm 101:5; Matthew 18:17; 1 Corinthians 5:5–6, 13). Paul wrote, "Now I beseech you, brethren, mark them which cause divisions and offenses contrary to the doctrine which ye have learned; and avoid them" (Romans 16:17). John Adams put it this way, "Never trouble trouble till trouble troubles you."[10] A wiser man still observed: "Make no friendship with an angry man; and with a furious man thou shalt not go: lest thou learn his ways, and get a snare to thy soul" (Proverbs 22:24). Lady Holland said, "Troubles are like babies; they grow larger by nursing."

We should give them a hard look (Proverbs 25:23). Discourage sin. Don't allow others to use you for a trash dump.

The emblem of the Commonwealth of Kentucky shows two men facing each other shaking hands. The motto beneath reads: "United we stand, divided we fall." That could well be the motto of a nation, a congregation, or a family. Church members are like coals in a fire. When we cling together, we keep the flame aglow; if we separate, we die out. One leader suggested, "None of us is as smart as all of us."[11]

❤❤

Questions to Consider and Discuss

1. What are the causes of most divisions among brethren?

2. Choose a statement to discuss further:
    a. Love would rather suffer wrong than do wrong (1 Corinthians 6:7).
    b. Some people just "love a good argument."
    c. "An ungodly man diggeth up evil: and in his lips there is as a burning fire" (Proverbs 16:27).
    d. "Envy is the only marksman that shoots at others and wounds herself."
    e. "A whisperer separateth chief friends" (Proverbs 16:28).
    f. "Never trouble trouble till trouble troubles you" (American proverb).
    g. "None of us is as smart as all of us."

3. What is the above-all-things doctrine of 1 Peter? How does it relate to sowing discord in the church?

4. "We should spend our zeal in the pursuit of the things that matter." What are some of the things that matter?

5. Explain how righteousness, peace, and joy are a good summary of Christianity (Romans 14:17).

6. What are some practical ways to handle someone who wants to sow seeds of discord in our ears?

CHAPTER TWELVE

THE DEVIL LOVES TO FISH IN TROUBLED WATERS

W hen the same royal family ruled both Spain and France, it was said, "There are no more Pyrenees." For centuries, those high mountains had divided the two nations, but a common king had overcome that geographic barrier.

When Christ our King brings us into His kingdom, the personal things that divide us fade into insignificance. Those who hope to be forgiven of God whom we have offended must be ready to forgive others.[1]

The Lord hates one that "soweth discord among brethren" (Proverbs 6:19), so it is safe to say that the devil loves to fish in troubled waters. In this chapter let us spend time pondering the value of harmony, the importance of the right kind of division, and the many benefits unity brings to individuals and churches.

THE INESTIMABLE VALUE OF PEACE AND HARMONY

The Holy Bible is a book about peace. It teaches man how to be at peace with his God, his neighbor, and himself (Philippians 4:6–7; Romans 12:18; 1 John 3:21). The word *peace* is used four hundred times in the Bible; *peaceable* is found eight times.[2]

Among these, the kingdom of Christ was prophesied to be a peaceable kingdom (Isaiah 11:6, 9). We are to pray that we may "lead a quiet and peaceable life in all godliness and honesty" (1 Timothy 2:2), and we should strive to be "one of them that are peaceable and faithful in Israel" (2 Samuel 20:19). Wisdom from above is first "peaceable" (James 3:17). Paul commanded, "Let us therefore follow after the things which make for peace, and things wherewith one may edify another" (Romans 14:19). One manifestation of bearing the fruit of the Spirit is peace (Galatians 5:22).

One of Jesus' beatitudes is: "Blessed are the peacemakers: for they shall be called the children of God" (Matthew 5:9). The Lord's kingdom is a kingdom of peace (Isaiah 2:1–4). We follow the "Prince of Peace" (Isaiah 9:6), who left peace with His disciples (John 14:27). We worship the God of peace (2 Thessalonians 3:16), and we are told to "follow peace" (Hebrews 12:14), "pursue peace" (1 Peter 3:11), and "live in" peace (2 Corinthians 13:11). We are commanded: "Be at peace among yourselves" (1 Thessalonians 5:13).

Notice God's words throughout time on this subject:
- "Seek peace and pursue it" (Psalm 34:14).
- "Have peace one with another" (Mark 9:50).
- "If it be possible, as much as lieth in you, live peaceably with all men" (Romans 12:18).
- "Let us therefore follow after the things which make for peace, and things wherewith one may edify another" (Romans 14:19).
- "Let him seek peace, and ensue it" (1 Peter 3:11).

There is no doubt that it is the responsibility of every child of God to do his best to keep peace in the body of Christ. Paul commanded us to endeavor "to keep the unity of the Spirit in the bond of peace" (Ephesians 4:3). The word "endeavor" (*spoudazo*) means "to use speed, i.e. to make effort, be prompt or earnest; give diligence, labour." While peace and unity cannot be had at the expense of truth, all people purchased by God should seek to live in peace and unity with their brethren.

The religious world is divided. Cartoonist Ed Koehler may have struck a nerve when he drew this cartoon: A preacher, on the phone: "Bad news, Bishop. Our church-planting team is divided on whether to call the new congregation 'First United Church' or 'United First Church.'"[3] Cartoonist Tim Liston quipped about another similar situation: "Officially, the results of the vote are forty 'yes,' seven 'no,' and one 'over my dead body.'"[4] One source reported the following:

- Number of Christian places of worship in the U.S.: 405,000.
- Number with no affiliation to any other group: 100,000.

Churches of Christ must carry the banner of brotherhood to a denominational—meaning divided—world. Brotherhood matters. Peter instructed us to "love the brotherhood" (1 Peter 2:17).

SCRIPTURAL DIVISION LEADS TO SCRIPTURAL UNITY

Despite the value that God places on peace and harmony, He requires certain kinds of division before we can be united with Him and with His people. The same Jesus who said, "Blessed are the peacemakers" also said,

> Suppose ye that I am come to give peace on earth? I tell you, Nay; but rather division: For from henceforth there shall be five in one house divided, three against two, and two against three. The father shall be divided against the son, and the son against the father; the mother against the daughter, and the daughter against the mother; the mother in law against her daughter in law, and the daughter in law against her mother in law (Luke 12:51–53).

Matthew had earlier recorded Jesus as saying,

> Think not that I am come to send peace on earth: I came not to send peace, but a sword. For I am come to set a man at variance against his father, and the daughter against her mother, and the daughter-in-law against her mother-in-law. And a man's foes shall be they of his own household. He that loveth father or mother more than me is not worthy of me: and he that loveth son or daughter more than me is not worthy of me (Matthew 10:34–37).

John records that His prediction came true: "So there was a division among the people because of him" (John 7:43; cf. 7:12; 9:16; 10:19). This continued in the early days of the church (Acts 14:4; 23:7–10), and continues in each generation.

By definition, the church is a group of "called out ones." We cannot gain membership in it until we sever our ties to the world (cf. James 4:4). Paul wrote,

> Wherefore come out from among them, and be ye separate, saith the Lord, and touch not the unclean thing; and I will receive you, and will be a Father unto you, and ye shall be my sons and daughters, saith the Lord Almighty (2 Corinthians 6:17–18).

Isaiah emphatically made this point to the people of his day: "Depart ye, depart ye, go ye out from thence, touch no unclean thing; go ye out of the midst of her; be ye clean, that bear the vessels of the Lord" (Isaiah 52:11).

During Korah's rebellion in the Old Testament, three times God told the righteous to separate from the unrighteous. For instance: "And he spake unto the congregation, saying, Depart, I pray you, from the tents of these wicked men, and touch nothing of theirs, lest ye be consumed in all their sins" (Numbers 16:26; cf. 16:21, 45; Jeremiah 51:6). Ezra demanded that those who repented "separate yourselves from the people of the land, and from the strange wives" (Ezra 10:11). The first verse of the most popular book in the Bible promises a blessing to the one who "walketh not in the counsel of the ungodly, nor standeth in the way of sinners, nor sitteth in the seat of the scornful" (Psalm 1:1).

Solomon himself said, "Forsake the foolish, and live; and go in the way of understanding" (Proverbs 9:6). Peter urged sinners with many words, saying, "Save yourselves from this untoward generation" (Acts 2:40). Paul exhorted Christians to the same course: "Having therefore these promises, dearly beloved, let us cleanse ourselves from all filthiness of the flesh and spirit, perfecting holiness in the fear of God" (2 Corinthians 7:1; cf. Ezra 6:21). John adds his voice to the chorus near the end of the Bible: "And I heard another voice from heaven, saying, Come out of her, my people, that ye be not partakers of her sins, and that ye receive not of her plagues" (Revelation 18:4).

Further, we are commanded: "Withdraw yourselves from every brother that walketh disorderly, and not after the tradition which he received of us" (2 Thessalonians 3:6; 1 Corinthians 5:11). Paul regulates our behavior toward such a brother: "And if any man obey not our word by this epistle, note that man, and have no company with him, that he may be ashamed. Yet count him not as an enemy, but admonish him as a brother" (2 Thessalonians 3:14–15; cf. Matthew 18:17).

Paul describes the type of person from whom we must withdraw:

> He is proud, knowing nothing, but doting about questions and strifes of words, whereof cometh envy, strife, railings, evil surmisings, perverse disputings of men of corrupt minds, and destitute of the truth, supposing that gain is godliness: from such withdraw thyself (1 Timothy 6:4–5).

> For men shall be lovers of their own selves, covetous, boasters, proud, blasphemers, disobedient to parents, unthankful, unholy, without natural affection, trucebreakers,

false accusers, incontinent, fierce, despisers of those that are good, traitors, heady, highminded, lovers of pleasures more than lovers of God; having a form of godliness, but denying the power thereof: from such turn away (2 Timothy 3:2–5).

Isaiah said, "There is no peace, saith my God, to the wicked" (Isaiah 57:21).

The psalmist urged, "Pray for the peace of Jerusalem: they shall prosper that love thee. Peace be within thy walls, and prosperity within thy palaces. For my brethren and companions' sakes, I will now say, Peace be within thee" (Psalm 122:6–8). Note his emphasis on unity for the sake of others. In one of Aesop's fables, two mountain goats met each other on a narrow ledge that was just wide enough for one animal to pass. On the left was a sheer cliff straight up, on the right, a deep lake far below. As the two faced each other, what should they do? It was too dangerous to back up. They could not turn around; the ledge was too narrow. If the goats had as little sense as people, they might have butted heads until one, or both, fell into the lake. But these goats had more horse sense than that. One laid down on the trail and let the other walk over him, and both were safe.

If two people had thought of this solution, they might still have argued about who would have to lie down. How often our stubbornness results in tragedy. We often hear, "I'm going to stand up for my rights!" or, "It is the principle of the thing I'm fighting for!" How hard it is to humble ourselves in the best interest of others. Jesus told us, "Don't resist evil, return good for evil," and, "Turn the other cheek, go the second mile" (cf. Matthew 5:38–41). He was saying a true Christian is strong enough to let another walk over him—to suffer wrong for the good of others. Someone copied this inscription off a tombstone:

> Here lies the body of Jonathan Gray
> who died maintaining his right of way.
> He was right, dead right, as he sped along.
> But he's just as dead as if he'd been wrong.

When we humble ourselves for the good of others, we show by our response that others do not control us—Christ does. There is nothing another can take from us that we would not freely give. Remember the lesson of the goat: It is better to allow ourselves to be walked over than to butt heads!

THE BENEFITS OF UNITY AMONG BRETHREN

Harmony helps the church grow faster—more people are saved (John 13:35). After D-Day in World War II, someone said to General Eisenhower, "It's great how you were able to coordinate all the teams in that great enterprise." The general quickly corrected him: "Not *teams*," he said, "but *team*."

That's what makes God's army successful, too. We will never become a church that effectively reaches out to those who are missing out if we shoot our wounded and major on the minuses. Instead of being fishers of men, we will be keepers of an ever-shrinking aquarium. If we are going to take the whole Gospel to the whole world in every generation, we need to network, integrate, coordinate, and cooperate. Aesop said, "United we stand, divided we fall." More important, Jesus said, "If a house be divided against itself, that house cannot stand" (Mark 3:25).

One man tested the strength of a glass beaker by successfully using it as a hammer to drive a nail into a wooden plank. Next he took a pea-sized marble and dropped it through the bottle's neck. When the marble hit the bottom, the glass container shattered. Although it was resistant to blows from the outside, the beaker was easily destroyed from within. The beautiful bride of Christ is like that. What atheists and enemies of truth could never do from the outside, selfish and shallow church members can do from within. The devil must laugh out loud when lost people are turned off by a bickering congregation.

Further, a united congregation produces an environment in which young Christians are built up, strengthened, and matured. Two men were riding a bicycle built for two when they came to a tall, steep hill. It took a great deal of struggle to complete what proved to be a very stiff climb. When they got to the top the man in front wiped his sweaty brow, turned to the other, and said, "Boy, that sure was a hard climb." The fellow in back replied, "Yes, and if I hadn't kept the brakes on we would have rolled down backwards."[5] Some churches have both guys on their rolls!

Harmony makes the church stronger—more good works are done. Thomas Carlyle said, "Ten men banded together in love and unity can do what ten thousand separately would fail to do."[6] Unity consistently produces greater results than individual endeavors. "Teamwork divides the effort and multiplies the effect."[7] David's peaceful son wrote: "A threefold cord is not quickly broken" (Ecclesiastes 4:12). Consider a couple of examples:

- Townspeople at a county fair held a horse-pulling contest. The first-place horse moved a sled weighing 4,500 pounds. The second-place finisher pulled 4,000 pounds. The owners of the two horses decided to see what these horses could pull together. They hitched them and found that the team could move

12,000 pounds. Working separately, the horses were good for only 8,500 pounds. Working together, their synergism produced an added 3,500 pounds.

- Next fall when you see geese heading south for the winter, flying along in V formation, you might be interested in knowing what science has discovered about why they fly that way. As each bird flaps its wings, it creates an uplift for the bird immediately following. By flying in a V formation, the whole flock adds at least 71 percent greater flying range than if each bird flew on its own. (Lesson: Christians who share a common direction and a sense of community can get where they are going quicker and easier).

Whenever a goose falls out of formation, it suddenly feels the drag and resistance of trying to go it alone and quickly gets back into formation to take advantage of the lifting power of the bird immediately in front. (Lesson: If we have as much sense as a goose, we will stay in formation with those who are headed the same way we are going). When the lead goose gets tired, he rotates back in the wing and another goose flies point. (Lesson: It pays to take turns doing hard jobs). The geese honk from behind to encourage those up front to keep up their speed. (Lesson: Encourage each other).

Finally, when a goose gets sick or wounded, two geese fall out of formation and follow him down to help and protect him. They stay with him until he is either able to fly or until he is dead, and then they launch out on their own or with another formation to catch up with their original group. (Lesson: If people knew we would stand by them like that in church, they would push down these walls to get in). We need to have as much sense as geese.[8]

Harmony helps the church avoid cliques and hurt feelings. Describing Bologna, Italy, a writer said, "Churches, of course, are everywhere and you can never quite discover which bell tower is ringing out the hour. There are churches within churches." He then describes churches that have been enlarged, rebuilt, and redesigned. The phrase "churches within churches" is interesting. God never intended for us to divide the church into competing cliques. All of us will have a circle of friends, usually based on our age, family situation, and interests, but we must never exclude or be antagonistic toward others (1 Corinthians 1:10–12).

Remember the *Maine*? The *Maine* was the U.S. battleship that got us into the Spanish-American War, not by the damage it did but by the damage that was done to it. When the news reported that a Spanish mine had sunk our ship in Havana Harbor, the now-famous war cry began that hurled us into war with Spain: "Remember the

Maine!" At 9:40 p.m. on February 15, 1898, the American battleship *Maine* exploded in the harbor of Havana, Cuba. There were 354 officers and men aboard; 266 lost their lives. The 300-foot vessel had been anchored at the same spot since late January. Her purpose had been to defend American interests during the civil war that Cuba was fighting against Spain.

There were three separate examinations of the wreckage. One was performed in connection with the 1898 United States court of inquiry. A second was performed by Spanish divers, also in 1898. And a third was performed in connection with the 1911 Board of Inspection and Survey. The first two inspections did little to shed light on what had happened.

The third probe in 1911 proved to be significant. A cofferdam was built. The water was removed from around the *Maine*. Every bit of the wreckage was accurately identified. Displacements were measured. Photographs were taken. The data was properly and carefully studied by experts. When experts observed the photographs of the wreckage, with hull sides and whole deck structures peeled back, it left no doubt. The explosion that sank our ship and catapulted us into the Spanish-American War was caused by a blast from twenty thousand pounds of powder . . . *from the inside.* God wants us to avoid internal explosions that may do damage to the old ship of Zion.

Harmony brings joy. The Polish border town of Cieszyn (pronounced che-shin) has an interesting name. It is a contraction of a Polish sentence that means "I am happy." According to legend, there were three brothers, long separated. They were reunited in this place and one said, "I am so happy," giving the town its name. It reminds us of Psalm 133:1 where the Bible says, "Behold, how good and how pleasant it is for brethren to dwell together in unity!"

Unity is good because it promotes harmony and cooperation. It is pleasant because it is charming and enjoyable. The Spirit hinted at this truth again in the Hebrews epistle: "Follow peace with all men, and holiness, without which no man shall see the Lord: looking diligently lest any man fail of the grace of God; lest any root of bitterness springing up trouble you, and thereby many be defiled" (Hebrews 12:14–15). A root of bitterness can both "trouble" (*enochleo*, "to crowd in, figurative to annoy"; the root means "to harass") and "defile" (*miaino*, "to sully or taint, contaminate") a Christian. In other words, it is evil—the opposite of good—and unpleasant.

Christianity brings joy; it has often been said that "the devil has no happy old men." Madalyn Murray O'Hair, the famous atheist, was interviewed on public television.

During the interview it was noted that Ms. O'Hair seemed to have a lot of clout. The interviewer asked why she didn't organize the atheist movement better to make it a stronger power. She responded, "Because every time a bunch of atheists get together, all they do is argue."[9]

Harmony brings God's blessings. A man went to an asylum for the criminally insane. He was a bit surprised to find that there were three guards taking care of a hundred inmates. He said to one, "Aren't you afraid that the inmates will unite, overcome you, and escape?"

The guard said, "Lunatics never unite."[10]

God said in the long ago: "How beautiful upon the mountains are the feet of him that bringeth good tidings, that publisheth peace; that bringeth good tidings of good, that publisheth salvation; that saith unto Zion, Thy God reigneth!" (Isaiah 52:7). Jesus said, "Blessed are the peacemakers: for they shall be called the children of God" (Matthew 5:9).

Harmony will one day enable us to see the Lord. Benjamin Franklin said, "We must all hang together, or we shall all hang separately." If we fail to maintain peace on earth, we will never enjoy the peace of heaven. Each Sunday, one minister presented a "children's sermon" to young children. A bright-eyed three-year-old girl listened intently as he explained that God wanted them all to get along and love each other. "God wants us all to be one," he said. The little girl replied, "But I don't want to be one. I want to be four!"[11]

Sometimes, we don't want to be one either, but the Bible is about community, from the Garden of Eden to the City at the end. Being one will lead us to the Promised Land: "Follow peace with all men, and holiness, without which no man shall see the Lord" (Hebrews 12:14). A story from church history illustrates the seriousness of obeying all God's commands—including those that relate to peace. At Antioch, two brothers had fallen out; after a while one desired to be reconciled, but the other refused. The persecution of Valerian began; Sapricius, the one who refused to forgive his brother, boldly confessed Christ and was being marched to his execution. Nicephorus met him, and again asked for peace, which was again refused. While one was seeking, and the other refusing, they arrived at the place of execution. He that should have been the martyr became terrified, offered to sacrifice to the gods, and despite the other's entreaties, forsook the Lord. Nicephorus, boldly confessing, stepped in his place and received the crown which Sapricius lost.[12]

Harmony keeps us in fellowship with the God of peace. "Be perfect, be of good comfort, be of one mind, live in peace; and the God of love and peace shall be with you" (2 Corinthians 13:11).

Questions to Consider and Discuss

1. What tricks do you think the devil uses to get Christians to argue with each other about insignificant things?

2. Explain how horses and geese working together show how Christians can get more done by cooperation.

3. Choose a statement to discuss further:
   a. We will never become a church that effectively reaches out to those who are missing out if we shoot our wounded and major on the minuses.
   b. "Behold, how good and how pleasant it is for brethren to dwell together in unity!" (Psalm 133:1).

4. Do you agree with the statement, "The devil has no happy old men"? Why do you think this is so, or not so?

5. What are some practical ways to gain the blessing promised to peacemakers? (Matthew 5:9).

CHAPTER THIRTEEN

THE BATTLEMENT OF GOD'S LOVE

Homeowners in Israel were required to construct a battlement on their roofs so no one would fall and "bring blood upon" the house (Deuteronomy 22:8). A *battlement* is defined as "parapet; a low wall at the edge of a balcony, roof, or along the sides of a bridge."[1] Their houses were usually built with flat roofs that were used much like we use porches or decks—sometimes even for exercise and sleeping (cf. Acts 10:9–10). Since people were often on roofs, it increased the likelihood that a careless child, rambunctious teenager, or teetering grandparent would fall over the edge. To prevent such accidents, God required barriers to make it harder for someone to be injured or killed.

We are familiar with barriers. National parks use guardrails to keep visitors from getting too close to the edge of dangerous cliffs. Zoos use rails, cages, and ditches to keep dangerous animals separated from too curious Homo sapiens. Highway departments block off roads that are flooded, have bridges washed out, or are under repair. Landowners seal up old wells with lumber or concrete to keep people from accidentally falling into them. Electric companies build high fences with sharp wire and red warning signs around places where one could be electrocuted. Such barricades are for our protection.

God also wants to protect us, especially from sin. He doesn't want us to fall prey to the seven sins He hates, so God built a battlement of love around the human family to protect us from falling off the earth into the lake of fire (John 3:16; Ephesians 2:8–9; 1 John 4:7–8). If we go into eternal Gehenna, we will have to crawl over, under, and around the love of God to get there.

The book of 1 John has love for its theme. There are one hundred five verses in the book, and love is mentioned forty-two times (about every third verse).[2] It tells us that "God is love" (1 John 4:8), and then shows that God has demonstrated ("made manifest") His love (3:16; 4:9–10). In 1 John 4:10–21 John gives three characteristics of God's love: It is personal, perfecting, and preserving.

GOD'S LOVE IS PERSONAL (1 JOHN 4:10–11)

Note the personal pronouns in John's two sentences: "Herein is love, not that we loved God, but that he loved us, and sent his Son to be the propitiation for our sins. Beloved, if God so loved us, we ought also to love one another." Sure, "God so loved *the world*" (John 3:16), but Jesus also loved *me*, and gave himself for *me* (Galatians 2:20). Someone said, "The love of God is one of the great realities of the universe, a pillar upon which the hope of the world rests. But it is a personal, intimate thing too. God does not love populations, He loves people. He loves not masses, but men."[3]

Someone wrote a piece called "God's Crazy About You," that illustrates the personal nature of God's love for us:

- If God had a refrigerator, your picture would be on it.
- If He had a wallet, your photo would be in it.
- He sends you flowers every spring and a sunrise every morning.
- Whenever you want to talk, He'll listen.
- He could live anywhere in the universe, but He chose your heart.
- What about the gift He sent you in Bethlehem; not to mention that Friday at Calvary!

GOD VALUES YOU

What can a God who owns everything (Psalm 50:10–12), knows everything (1 John 3:20), and can do everything (Jeremiah 32:17, 27) value? God treasures you—His faithful child! Even though we are all unprofitable servants (Luke 17:10), God considers us precious (Revelation 14:13). We are always on His mind.

God had you in mind since the world's creation.

> Blessed be the God . . . who hath blessed us with all spiritual blessings in heavenly
> places in Christ: according as he hath chosen us in him before the foundation of
> the world, that we should be holy and without blame before him in love: having
> predestinated us unto the adoption of children by Jesus Christ to himself, accord-
> ing to the good pleasure of his will (Ephesians 1:3–5).

This is "according to the eternal purpose which he purposed in Christ" (Ephesians 3:11).

God predestinated that each person could be saved in the church. Carefully notice the
text says that all blessings are in Christ and that we are chosen in him. To be in Christ is
to be in His body, the church (Galatians 3:26–27; Ephesians 1:22–23; 4:4). If you had
been the only one who would have ever accepted the invitation to come into Christ, God
would still have developed this beautiful scheme of redemption. He loves each one indi-
vidually as much as He does the world collectively (Romans 5:8; John 3:16).

It is exciting to study history in light of God's providential working to bring His saving
plan to pass. Since man's fall (Genesis 3), God has been working to see him restored—
beginning at Genesis 3:15. He promised Abraham a descendant (Christ) who would
bless all nations (Genesis 12:1–3; Galatians 3:16–17). He produced the nation of Israel
through which the Messiah would be born (Exodus). He gave them property (Joshua)
and instruction (the prophets). He kept the seed line pure (1 Kings–2 Chronicles) so
that Christ was born of the seed of Abraham and the lineage of David (2 Samuel
7:12–16; Matthew 1; Luke 3).

He brought about the virgin birth and protected the innocent child from wicked rulers
(Matthew 1–2). He raised the crucified Lamb from the grave and set Him on heaven's
throne (Mark 16; Romans 1:4; 1 Corinthians 15:1–4). He established the church—the
Messiah's kingdom—into which all men may flow and be saved (Isaiah 2:1–4; Acts 2).
Yes, it can be safely said that God values you!

God had you in mind when Jesus was sent. When God thought of you and the
dilemma your sin had caused, He decided to empty heaven of its most precious jewel
so you could be saved (2 Corinthians 8:9). The only way God could be the justifier of
man and remain just in character was to substitute the free offering of a perfect sacrifice. Christ was the only such offering.

> Being justified freely by his grace through the redemption that is in Christ Jesus:
> whom God hath set forth to be a propitiation through faith in his blood, to declare

his righteousness for the remission of sins that are past through the forbearance of God; to declare . . . at this time his righteousness: that he might be *just, and the justifier* of him which believeth in Jesus (Romans 3:24–26).

We generally value something by how much we must pay for it. Since God paid for you and the church with His Son's blood (Ephesians 1:7; Acts 20:28), consider how much He values you as an individual member of the church! "He that spared not his own Son, but delivered him up for us all, how shall he not with him also freely give us all things?" (Romans 8:32). Yes, God values you!

God has you in mind now. You are not forgotten and left to sink or swim on your own. God is still interested (1 Peter 5:7). Jesus encouraged,

> Ask, and it shall be given you; seek, and ye shall find; knock, and it shall be opened unto you: for everyone that asketh receiveth; and he that seeketh findeth; and to him that knocketh it shall be opened. . . . if ye then being evil, know how to give good gifts unto your children, how much more shall your Father which is in heaven give good things to them that ask him? (Matthew 7:7–11).

YOU ARE TREASURED!

God will have you in mind at the judgment day. As one of those who has washed His robe in the blood of the Lamb by being baptized into Christ (Revelation 7:14; Acts 22:16), your name is written on heaven's roll (Philippians 4:3), and will be read at Judgment Day (Revelation 22:12). At the final day, after a faithful life (Revelation 2:10), your ears will hear the sweet words, "Come, ye blessed of my Father, inherit the kingdom prepared for you from the foundation of the world" (Matthew 25:34).

God has used some creative and interesting ways to express His love for us. Consider these ideas.

Hairs and Birds. Every individual person is important to God, and He loves each one. Jesus said,

> Are not five sparrows sold for two farthings, and not one of them is forgotten before God? But even the very hairs of your head are all numbered. Fear not therefore: ye are of more value than many sparrows. Also I say unto you, whosoever shall confess me before men, him shall the Son of man also confess before the angels of God (Luke 12:6–8).

Isn't that amazing!? No little bird can have a heart attack and fall from the sky without God noticing. No sparrow can go to sleep one night in its nest and never wake up and God not think, "One of my creatures has died." How much more important does God count His own children than a dead bird?

God knows every hair on our heads, which is something that most of us don't even know about ourselves. (Just for the record, the average head has about 100,000 hair follicles.) God loves us and He knows everything about us. His love can therefore be intimate, personal, one-of-a-kind. There are no don't-go-theres or hidden secrets to keep out of view. There are no facades or pretenses. God knows who we are, where we've been, and what resides deepest in our hearts.

A Divine Pedometer and Tears in a Bottle. God not only numbers our hairs, but also our steps and our tears. In recounting the heart-breaking episodes of being hounded from place to place by King Saul, David says: "Thou numberest my wanderings" (Psalm 56:8). David knew the Lord had watched as he had been driven relentlessly into hiding and then from place to place. A divine pedometer had numbered every step. Jehovah was aware of all the dangers confronting David. To borrow Job's words, David might well have asked: "Does he not see my ways, and number all my steps?" (Job 31:4).

David continued to implore God, saying, "Put thou my tears in thy bottle" (Psalm 56:8). He begged his Maker to remember his tears—treasure them up as men might preserve costly liquids. God will do exactly that for each of us. This reminds us of God's comforting words to King Hezekiah: "I have heard thy prayers, I have seen thy tears" (2 Kings 20:5). Is it not wonderful to know, when our hearts are heavy with sorrow, that there is One who is never too busy to care? Others may not notice our heartaches, but God always does (2 Corinthians 1:3; 1 Peter 5:7). Therefore, "Cast thy burden upon the LORD, and he will sustain thee" (Psalm 55:22).

Sheep and Cows. Jesus illustrated the personal nature of divine love by comparing it to a shepherd's relationship with his flock. He said, "I am the good shepherd, and know my sheep, and am known of mine. As the Father knoweth me, even so know I the Father: and I lay down my life for the sheep" (John 10:14–15). A good shepherd in Bible times knew each sheep by sight, and usually by name.

This may not connect with most Americans as well as a cattle illustration. Imagine a boy growing up on a ranch. You drive by the ranch and see only a herd of Angus cattle grazing in the pasture. They all look the same to you—but not to that young man. He remembers the night when this one was born. He remembers when that one was bought at the cattle sale. And that one over there? Well, he's the mean one you don't turn your back on. That big one stepped on his foot once and left him hobbling for three days. They are all individuals to him, because he has been around them so much.

To God, we are all individuals. He remembers us from when we were just children. He loves us in spite of knowing our every weakness, mistake, inadequacy, shortcoming, flaw, and quirk. One speaker theorized: "I think if our children knew how much we loved them, they couldn't handle it." I'm not sure of that, but I'm confident that if we really knew how much God loves us and is personally involved in our day-to-day lives, we couldn't handle it. We'd feel embarrassed, intimidated, undone, and unworthy (cf. Isaiah 6:5); but God wants us to feel loved, wanted, embraced, accepted, and valued.

Pigs and Only Children. The pot-bellied-pigs craze of the 1980s eventually left a lot of orphaned porkers, unwanted by their owners. Dan Riffle came to the rescue, adopting the unwanted pigs on his five-acre farm, which was virtually "hog heaven."[4] We might wonder how someone could love pigs so much, but what is more amazing is how a holy, perfect God can love sinful people so much (Romans 5:6–10).

The Bible tells us that God not only loves us but that He also wants to adopt us into His family (Romans 8:15, 23; Galatians 4:5; Ephesians 1:5). He wants us to call Him Father (Matthew 23:9; cf. 6:9). Consider the honor of that! Augustine said, "He loves each one of us, as if there were only one of us." God is not limited as we are as parents. We have only so much time, energy, talent, patience, and money to spend on our children. If we have several children, they may sometimes feel they would like to be an only child. God has unlimited resources (Psalm 50:10; Philippians 4:19), so He can literally treat each of His millions of children as an only child.

GOD'S LOVE IS PERFECTING (4:12)

God's love is perfect—any modification would take away from it (Deuteronomy 32:4). Psalm 103:8–12 speaks of the perfection of God's love. It says that God has:

- A long fuse: "The LORD is merciful and gracious, slow to anger, and plenteous in mercy" (103:8).

- A short memory: "He will not always chide: neither will he keep his anger for ever" (103:9).

- A thick skin: "He hath not dealt with us after our sins; nor rewarded us according to our iniquities" (103:10).

- A big heart: "For as the heaven is high above the earth, so great is his mercy toward them that fear him. As far as the east is from the west, so far hath he removed our transgressions from us" (103:11–12).

It is interesting that the psalmist chose east and west instead of north and south to illustrate God's heart. On a globe, if you go north, you will eventually reach the North Pole, and if you keep walking in a straight line, you will start heading south. This is not so with traveling east or west. If one goes east around the globe, he never reaches west. Like the distance between east and west, God's love cannot be measured (Ephesians 3:19).

Principle. Since God's love is perfect, the phrase "His love is perfected in us" must have to do with perfecting us. Love always seeks to improve the object of its delight. A friend "sharpens" his friend (Proverbs 27:17). Good parents constantly mold, mind, and mentor their offspring (Genesis 18:19; Proverbs 22:6). Spouses teach each other God's Word (1 Corinthians 14:35; Acts 18:26), encourage each other's strong points, shore up each other's weak points, and grow together (cf. Luke 1:6).

In a similar way, God perfects his love in us. "The LORD will perfect that which concerneth me: thy mercy, O LORD, endureth for ever: forsake not the works of thine own hands" (Psalm 138:8). He set teachers in the church for the "perfecting of the saints" (Ephesians 4:12). He sanctifies and cleanses "with the washing of water by the word" (Ephesians 5:26). He makes us perfect, stablishes, strengthens, settles us (1 Peter 5:10).

Illustration:

- As a Silversmith, God sits "as a refiner and purifier of silver: and he shall purify the sons of Levi, and purge them as gold and silver, that they may offer unto the LORD an offering in righteousness" (Malachi 3:3).

- As a Potter, He makes of us what He wants (Isaiah 64:8). We are His workmanship (Ephesians 2:10).

- As the Groom's Father, He wants the bride (the church) to be absolutely beautiful on her wedding day, "that he might present it to himself a glorious church, not having spot, or wrinkle, or any such thing; but that it should be holy and without blemish" (Ephesians 5:27).

- As a caring Teacher, He "rebukes and chastens" His students that they may graduate with honors (Revelation 3:19; cf. Proverbs 3:12).

- As a holy God, He wants to make us wholly holy[5] (1 Thessalonians 5:23).

- As a King, He intends to "purify unto himself a peculiar people, zealous of good works" (Titus 2:14).

- As the Master Manager of the Universe He works all things "together for good to them that love God, to them who are the called according to his purpose" (Romans 8:28).

A. W. Tozer said, "With the goodness of God to desire our highest welfare, the wisdom of God to plan it, and the power of God to achieve it, what do we lack?" Someone else wrote this thoughtful piece:

I asked God to take away my pride. And God said, "No." He said it was not for Him to take away, but for me to give up.

I asked God to make my handicapped child whole. And God said, "No." He said her spirit was whole; her body was only temporary.

I asked God to grant me patience. And God said, "No." He said patience is a by-product of tribulations. It isn't granted; it is earned.

I asked God to give me happiness. And God said, "No." He said He gives me blessings; happiness is up to me.

I asked God to make my spirit grow. And God said, "No." He said I must grow on my own. But He prunes me to make me fruitful.

I asked for all things that I might enjoy life. And God said, "No." He said, "I will give you life, that you may enjoy all things."

I asked God to help me love others as much as He loves me. And God said, "Ah, finally you have the idea."[6]

Application. Another way to translate the phrase "His love is perfected in us" is, "God's love completes us." What a wonderful thought! Without His love we can never be complete, but with it, all the pieces fall into place. Paul said, "And ye are complete in him, which is the head of all principality and power" (Colossians 2:10). Christ is all to us (Colossians 3:11). John wrote, "And of his fulness have all we received, and grace for grace" (John 1:16). Paul added, "That in every thing ye are enriched by him, in all utterance, and in all knowledge." "But of him are ye in Christ Jesus, who of God is made unto us wisdom, and righteousness, and sanctification, and redemption" (1 Corinthians 1:5, 30). "Being enriched in every thing to all bountifulness, which causeth through us thanksgiving to God" (2 Corinthians 9:11).

No other relationship can make us complete. Teens think, "If I can just get a girlfriend (boyfriend), I'll be whole." But they find that boyfriends (girlfriends) usually take one on a roller coaster of highs and lows—usually ending on the latter. Many college students and singles feel if they could just meet "Mr. Right" or "Miss Girl-of-My-Dreams," marry, and settle into a house with two cars and a mortgage, life would be complete. But it isn't. Then they think if they could just have a child, life would be perfect. But it isn't.

George Matheson understood this. He was only fifteen when he was told that he was losing his eyesight. Not to be denied, he enrolled in the University of Glasgow, and, despite failing sight, graduated at nineteen. As he pursued graduate studies in theology he did become blind. His sisters joined ranks beside him, learning Greek and Hebrew to assist him in his studies. He pressed faithfully on. But his spirit collapsed when his fiancée, unwilling to be married to a blind man, broke their engagement. He never married, and the pain of that rejection never totally left him. Years later, his sister announced her engagement. He rejoiced with her, but his mind went back to his own heartache. He consoled himself in thinking of God's love which is never limited, never conditional, never withdrawn, and never uncertain. Out of this experience he wrote the hymn, "O Love That Wilt Not Let Me Go."[7]

> O love that will not let me go,
> I rest my weary soul in thee;
> I give thee back the life I owe,
> That in thine ocean depths its flow,
> May richer, fuller be.

GOD'S LOVE IS PRESERVING (4:14)

A young boy fell into a deep West Texas well during a rainstorm. By the time his father found him, the rising water was almost to his neck. Unable to find anything to pull him out, the father jumped into the well and sent others to get help. When they finally returned, the rain and rising water had stopped. The father had drowned, but he still held his living son as high above his head as he could reach, which was just above the water level. His grip was so strong that rescuers literally had to pry the boy from his father's hands. Jim Schinnerer's story illustrates what God, through Jesus, did for us. When the waters of our sin were rising above our heads, Jesus came down from heaven to rescue us. Only His hands were stretched out on a cruel cross rather than above His head.[8]

We are saved to the uttermost. God wants every person on earth "to be saved, and to come unto the knowledge of the truth" (1 Timothy 2:4). That's why Jesus came to die (John 3:16). God did not send His Son to die on the cross just to prove that He loved us, but to save us. "For God sent not his Son into the world to condemn the world; but that the world through him might be saved" (John 3:17). God's love did not save us just to see us lost again. He wants to transport us safely through this world to heaven. He is "able also to save them to the uttermost[9] that come unto God by him, seeing he ever liveth to make intercession for them" (Hebrews 7:25).

Any work that God begins, He will finish. He told Samuel, "When I begin, I will also make an end" (1 Samuel 3:12). Of course, we can foil His plans by going back into sin (cf. 2 Peter 2:20–22) or refusing to submit to His Word, but if we will be faithful to Him, He will be faithful to us (Hebrews 10:23).

Paul was "confident[10] of this very thing, that he which hath begun a good work in you will perform it until the day of Jesus Christ" (Philippians 1:6). The word *perform*[11] means that God will carry it forward to completion. Barnes notes that it is an intensive form of the word, meaning that it would definitely be carried through to the end. The word occurs nowhere else in the New Testament. God will not leave His work—us!—unfinished. It would not be commenced and then abandoned. Vance Havner said, "This is the victory that overcomes the world when we are shipwrecked on God and stranded on Omnipotence!"

At the 1992 Olympics in Barcelona, in the 400-meter race Derek Redman tore a hamstring on the backstretch and sprawled on the track. He struggled to his feet and began hopping toward the finish line. His father bounded out of the stands, embraced his son, and said, "Come on, Son, let's finish this together."

God desires for us to make it to heaven, and He says to us all along the way, "Let's finish this together." He wants to preserve us—to save us and bring us home. God's love will last as long as God lasts (Psalm 90:2). He will not lose interest in us, or become fickle and turn against us. A wife may stop loving her husband, or vice versa, but God's love will never change toward us (James 1:17; Malachi 3:6). He will "never leave thee, nor forsake thee" (Hebrews 13:5). He loves lukewarm Christians who have forsaken Him. He loves every sinner on death row. A sinner may go to hell unsaved, but none will go there unloved!

We are kept. Peter said that the Lord is "not willing that any should perish" (2 Peter 3:9) and that we "are kept by the power of God through faith unto salvation ready to be revealed in the last time" (1 Peter 1:5). "Underneath [us] are the everlasting arms" (Deuteronomy 33:27). There shall be nothing lacking on God's part to support us and to bring us at last to His kingdom and glory. Since we are a part of the church built upon a rock, and the gates of Hades shall not prevail against it (Matthew 16:18), then God will do all in His power—short of trumping our free will—to keep the gates of Hades from prevailing against us.

We are unpluckable.

> My sheep hear my voice, and I know them, and they follow me: and I give unto them eternal life; and they shall never perish, neither shall any man pluck them out of my hand. My Father, which gave them me, is greater than all; and no man is able to pluck them out of my Father's hand (John 10:27–29).

The devil can lure us away from God (James 1:12–15), but if we stay close to God, neither he—nor any evil person—has the power to overcome us.

We are guarded. Jude said we are "sanctified by God the Father, and preserved in Jesus Christ, and called" (Jude 1). He knew that God was "able to keep you from falling, and to present you faultless before the presence of his glory with exceeding joy" (Jude 1:24). The words *preserved*[12] and *keep*[13] in these verses are similar. *Preserved* means "to guard from loss or injury by keeping the eye upon." *Keep* means "to watch, be on guard, preserve."

Naturalist S. L. Bastian once wrote of a spider he observed that builds its nest in the branch of a small tree or bush. In this delicate enclosure, baby spiders are hatched. If the nest is disturbed in any way, the little spiders rush out in fright. At once the mother goes to their side. She is alerted to their potential danger in a most unique way. Each of the young ones has a thin silky strand attached to it, and all of these strands are joined to the body of the mother. When the babies are threatened by an enemy, they naturally scurry off, giving their lines a sharp tug. This is instantly felt by the adult spider, and within seconds she pulls them back to the nest where they are protected from harm.

The prophet Hosea says that we are linked to God with cords of love, cords that cannot be broken (Hosea 11:4). The gentle cords of His eternal love bind all our hearts to Him and alert Him to our hurts. God is our "very present help in trouble" (Psalm 46:1). Tie this thought to Paul's: "God is faithful, who will not suffer you to be tempted above that ye are able; but will with the temptation also make a way to escape, that ye may be able to bear it" (1 Corinthians 10:13). When we are ready to flee from the dangers of sin and Satan, our God and Father will be right there, ready to save us from death and give the gift of eternal salvation.

Think of the greatness of divine love! All the love shared between all the husbands and wives who ever lived, all the love mothers and fathers who ever lived have felt for their babies, all the love expressed in all the acts of human kindness since the world began, all the tears of love shed in every funeral from the beginning of time, added together and multiplied times infinity, is not comparable to the love God feels for the vilest, most reprobate sinner who ever lived!

Questions to Consider and Discuss

1. In what ways did Jesus show His love for others while He was on the earth?

2. Choose a statement to discuss further:
    a. If God had a refrigerator, your picture would be on it.
    b. God loves us in spite of knowing our every weakness, mistake, inadequacy, shortcoming, flaw, and quirk.
    c. God wants us to feel loved, wanted, embraced, accepted, and valued.
    d. He loves each one of us, as if there were only one of us (Augustine).
    e. God will not lose interest in us.
    f. A sinner may go to hell unsaved, but none will go there unloved!
    g. Even though we are all unprofitable servants (Luke 17:10), God considers us precious (Revelation 14:13).

3. What is a battlement, and how does it relate to God's love?

4. Since we generally value something by how much we must pay for it, how much did God value the church?

5. How does God's love make us complete in a way that nothing else can?

6. What is the significance to comparing the love of God to east and west instead of north and south? (Psalm 103:12).

7. How does God "keep us from falling"? (Jude 24). Is it possible to fall from grace?

CHAPTER NOTES

Chapter 1

[1] Scott R. Bayles, "God Is Love," http://sermoncentral.com/.

[2] Gary Chapman, *The Five Languages of Love: How to Express Heartfelt Commitment to Your Mate*, Reprint ed. (Chicago: Moody Publishers, 1996).

[3] *sunistemi*, "to set together, that is (by implication) to introduce (favorably), or (figuratively) to exhibit; intransitively to stand near, or (figuratively) to constitute."

Chapter 2

[1] James S. Hewett, *Illustrations Unlimited* (Wheaton: Tyndale House Publishers, Inc, 1988), 295.

[2] Pride, 49; proud, 48 times; arrogancy, 4 times.

[3] *tuphoo*, used in 1 Timothy 6:4, for instance.

[4] *Merriam-Webster's Collegiate Dictionary*, 10th ed. (Springfield, MA: Merriam Webster, 1993).

[5] W. E. Vine and Merrill F. Unger, *Merrill F. Vine's Complete Expository Dictionary of Old and New Testament Words: With Topical Index* (Nelson Reference, 1996).

[6] "Martin Luther—The Early Years," *Christian History*, no. 34. (Christianity Today International).

[7] *huperephanos*.

[8] Hewett, p. 438.

[9] As quoted in Bob Phillips, *Phillips' Book of Great Thoughts & Funny Sayings* (Wheaton, IL: Tyndale House Publishers, Inc., 1993), 54.

[10] Vern McLellan, *The Complete Book of Practical Proverbs and Wacky Wit* (Wheaton: Tyndale House Publishers, Inc., 1996).

[11] Robert C. Shannon, *1000 Windows* (Cincinnati, Ohio: Standard Publishing Company, 1997).

[12] Note how *pride* and *foolishness* go together.

[13] Shannon.

[14] Those who are new Christians.

[15] Shannon.

[16] Shannon.

[17] Plutarch.

[18] Hewett, p. 296.

Chapter 3

[1] Thanks to Luke Griffin for internet research assistance.

[2] Dan Vess, "Does God Justify Deception?" *The Gospel Observer*. September 26, 1999.

[3] Charles V. Ford, *Lies! Lies!! Lies!!!* (Arlington: American Psychiatric Press, 1996).

[4] Josh King, "Lying: Our Favorite National Pastime." *The Cavalier Daily*. February 24, 1998.

[5] The study was conducted by Dr. Bella DePaulo, described in Allison Kornet, The Truth about Lying, *Psychology Today*, Vol. 30 Issue 3 (May/June 1997), 53.

[6] http://nlag.net/Sermons/Transcripts/mjdeadmendont.htm.

[7] Ibid.

[8] Things You Oughta Know About . . . A Top 10 Fact Sheet on Lies (for teens);
http://teenadvice.about.com/library/bl10thingslies.htm.

[9] "Everyone Loves a Liar," by Claudine Chamberlain, ABCNews.com http://more.abcnews.go.com/sections/
living/dailynews/lying0220.html.

[10] http://bankrate.com/brm/news/biz/thumb/20010117a.asp.

[11] *The Plain Truth* (Sept/Oct, 2003), 7.

[12] Adapted from: Phillips, John. *Exploring Proverbs*, Volume 1 (John Phillips Commentary Series). Kregel
Academic & Professional (2002).

[13] A social psychologist at the University of Massachusetts.

[14] Things You Oughta Know About . . . A Top 10 Fact Sheet.

[15] http://brainyquote.com/quotes/quotes/a/aldoushuxl101819.html.

[16] Orlando Clayton Lambert, *Catholicism Against Itself* (Grapevine, TX: Star Bible Publications), 35–36.

[17] *Health*, Vol. 17 Issue 1 (Jan/Feb 2003), 91.

[18] http://geocities.com/Athens/Forum/3505/kids.html. Adlai Stevenson is also credited with saying, "A lie is an
abomination unto the Lord, and a very present help in trouble."

[19] Things You Oughta Know About . . . A Top 10 Fact Sheet . . .

[20] "And Now, the Lying Game. From Clinton to Archer, the Combination of Charm and Deceit is Powerful"
by David Graham, Life Writer, *Toronto Star*, July 23, 2001.

[21] Cleon Lyles, *Wish I'd Said That*. 1969.

[22] Source: "How to Deal with Deception: Everybody Tells Fibs, But Outright Lying Is a Dead End Road in
Business." http://geocities.com/athens/forum/1611/sins22lies17.html.

[23] *Health,* Vol. 17 Issue 1 (Jan/Feb 2003), 91.

[24] Things You Oughta Know About . . . A Top 10 Fact Sheet . . .

Chapter 4

[1] Thanks to Luke Griffin for internet research assistance. U.S. Federal Bureau of Investigation, Crime in the
United States, Annual Report. See also http://fbi.gov/ucr/cius00/contents.pdf (released 15 October 2001).

[2] U.S. deaths in every American war up through Gulf War I: 620,219 deaths in combat; 950,851 related
deaths (non-combat); three wars not known; 1,560,584 wounded.

[3] Civilians killed by governments in the twentieth century, excluding war (in millions):

Soviet Union	62 million	1917–1991
China (Communist)	35 million	1949–Present
Germany	21 million	1933–45
China (Kuomintang)	10 million	1928–49
Japan	6 million	1936–45

Total deaths (excluding official wars) 170 million in the twentieth century.

"Statistics of Democide," by Rudy J. Rummel (With *The Economist* additions for recent wars).

[4] The Hebrew word for "kill" is *ratsach*. It can also be translated, "murder or slay." According to Strong, the
word translated "kill" in Exodus 20:13 is found 47 times in Scripture and is translated "slayer" (16), "murderer" (14), "kill" (5), "murder" (3), "slain" (3), "manslayer" (2), "killer" (1), "slayers" (1), "slayeth" (1),
"death" (1).

[5] Smiting (*nakah*) means "to beat, murder, slaughter."

[6] Jim Dethmer, "The Profit of Financial Integrity," *Seeds Tape Ministry,* February 21, 1993.

Chapter 5

[1] Incidentally, the killing of animals is not forbidden (Genesis 9:3). We have permission to take life from everything God created except people (Genesis 9:5–6).

[2] William Barclay, *The Ten Commandments for Today*, Reprint 1998 (Westminster: John Knox Press 1973).

[3] *The Ten Commandments for Today*, (Grand Rapids: Wm. B. Eerdmann's Pub. Co., 1973), 70–71.

[4] The words "shed" and "blood" are found in the same verse 46 times in Scripture (38 in the Old Testament; 8 in the New Testament).

Chapter 6

[1] John McClintock, *Cyclopedia of Biblical Theological and Ecclesiastical Literature*. (Baker Academic, 1982).

[2] Morris Fishbein, *The New Illustrated Medical and Health Encyclopedia* (H. S. Stuttman Co., 1975).

[3] Norman L. Geisler, *Christian Ethics, Options and Issues* (Baker Publishing Group, 1989).

[4] Spoken at the National Memorial of the Unborn dedication, March 23, 1997.

[5] *U.S. News and World Report*, March 4, 1974, p. 44.

[6] http://guttmacher.org/.

[7] AGI, "Parental involvement, State Policies in Brief," December 2002.

[8] S. K. Henshaw and K. Kost, "Parental Involvement in Minors' Abortion Decisions," *Family Planning Perspectives,* 24 (1992), (5):196–207, 213.

[9] These statistics are found at http://guttmacher.org/pubs/fb_induced_abortion.html#ref21 #ref21.

[10] "Call evil good" in Hebrew is literally, "say concerning evil, It is good."

[11] R. K. Jones, J. E. Darroch and S. K. Henshaw, "Patterns in the Socioeconomic Characteristics of Women Obtaining Abortions in 2000–2001, *Perspectives on Sexual and Reproductive Health,* 34 (2002), (5):226–235.

[12] "Pulpit Helps," Vol. 13, No. 4 (January 1988).

[13] *astorgos*, "from G1 (as a neg. particle) and a presumed derivative of *stergo* (to cherish affectionately); hard-hearted towards kindred; without natural affection."

[14] AGI, "State Funding of Abortion Under Medicaid*," State Policies in Brief* (December 2002).

[15] AK, AZ, CA, CT, HI, IL, MA, MD, MN, MT, NJ, NM, NY, OR, VT, WA, and WV.

[16] J. D. Forrest and R. Samara, "Impact of Publicly Funded Contraceptive Services on Unintended Pregnancies and Implications for Medicaid Expenditures, *Family Planning Perspectives,* 28 (1996), (5): 188–195.

[17] http://nrlc.org/news/2003/NRL02/cost.html.

[18] 1/8/90.

[19] 1/22/95.

[20] R. K. Jones, J. E. Darroch, and S. K. Henshaw, 2002, op. cit. (see reference 11).

[21] Sarah Terzo, http://gargaro.com/abortquotes.html.

[22] For instance, K. L. Moore's "The Developing Human, Clinically Oriented Embryology" 3rd edition, 1982.

[23] Unless otherwise noted, these are from: http://gospelweb.net/abortionquotes.htm. Some on the site were considered too gruesome to be included here.

[24] http://gargaro.com/abortquotes.html.

Chapter 7

[1] *Supreme Court Reporter*, 1973. Even the 1973 *Roe v. Wade* Supreme Court decision allowing abortion did not allow for the "my body" argument. It gave a woman the rights to privacy and abortion if there was perceived danger to her. It did not give unlimited rights to do with her body as she pleased.

[2] Charles Swindoll, *Sanctity of Life: The Inescapable Issue* (W. Pub Group: 1990).

[3] Swindoll.

[4] Dr. R. J. Hefferman of Tufts University, speaking before the Congress of American College of Surgeons (1957).

[5] E. Lenoski, *Heartbeat*, vol. 3, no. 4 (Dec., 1980).

[6] J. Walsh, IL Dept. of Child and Family Services, *Newsweek* (July 24, 1972). Not much has changed since these earlier investigations.

[7] If the woman goes directly to the hospital, her word is accepted as enough proof of rape. Reporting the rape to a law enforcement agency is needed and any hospital emergency room will handle this. If done within a day or two, she can be examined, given medicine for sexually transmitted diseases and counseled. Sadly, through fright or ignorance, the average rape victim does not report it. She quietly nurses her fears. She misses her period and hopes against hope that it isn't what she thinks it is. Sometimes months go by before finally, in tears, she reports to her mother, her physician, or some other counselor or confidante. To prove rape at that point is impossible. The only proof of rape then is to have a reliable witness corroborate the story, and such a witness almost never exists.

[8] S. Makhorn, in Mall & Watts, eds., "Sexual Assault & Pregnancy," *New Perspectives on Human Abortion*, (Washington, D.C.: University Publications of America, 1981), 58.

[9] AGI Website.

[10] *Post* (September 9, 1987).

[11] From a review of two separate studies, Dr. Charles M. Jarrett.

[12] M. Uchtman, Director, *Suiciders Anonymous*, Report to Cincinnati City Council, September 1, 1981.

[13] Video, *Pro-Life Doctors Speak Out*, (Cleveland, OH: American Portrait Films Inc., 1986).

[14] In a two-year period, 26 with legal abortions and 14 with spontaneous abortions.

[15] If one has symptoms of Post-Abortion Syndrome, she can call 1-800-5-WE-CARE (National Office of Post-abortion Reconciliation and Healing).

[16] Mahkorn, "Pregnancy & Sexual Assault." In *Psychological Aspects of Abortion*, (University Publishers of America, 1979), 53–72.

[17] Mahkorn and Dona, "Sexual Assault & Pregnancy." In *New Perspectives on Human Abortion*, (University Publishers of America, 1981), 182–199, Mahkorn, "Pregnancy & Sexual Assault." *In Psychological Aspects of Abortion*, 53–72.

[18] "Considering the prevalence of teenage pregnancies in general, incest treatment programs marvel at the low incidence of pregnancy from incest." Several reports agree at 1% or less. G. Maloof, "The Consequences of Incest," *The Psychological Aspects of Abortion*, (University Publications of America, 1979), 74–245.

[19] H. Maisch, *Incest,* (New York: Stein and Day Publishers, 1972).

[20] G. Maloof, "The Consequences of Incest," *The Psychological Aspects of Abortion,* (University Publications of America, 1979), 100.

[21] Dr. Bernard Nathanson, 73 at the time, a co-founder of the National Abortion and Reproductive Rights Action League, a leading pro-life advocate.

[22] P. Singer, "Sanctity of Life or Quality of Life?" *Pediatrics*, vol. 73, no. 1, (July 1983): 128–129.

[23] "Children from the Laboratory," J. Watson, *AMA Prism,* Ch. 3, p. 2 (May 1973).

[24] via *Hillcrest News*, Neosho, Missouri (via *Daily Bread* email, 12/30/03). http://cold-harbor-road.org/bread.htm.

[25] Blumberg et al, "Psychiatric Sequelae of Abortion for Genetic Indication," *American Journal OB/GYN,* vol. 122, no. 7, (Aug. 1975): 779–780.

[26] For information on where abortions are done close to you, see the Planned Parenthood website (http://ppalabama.org/sites.htm) or go to http://abortion.com. Interestingly, abortion is still illegal in some

states, as the law has never been changed; however, it is not enforced, since the law is now "unconstitutional," according to the *Encyclopedia of Abortion*.

Chapter 8

[1] This word (*logismos*, "computation, reasoning") is from the root *logizomai*, "to take an inventory, i.e. estimate (lit. or fig.); conclude."

[2] *chashab*, "to weave or fabricate; to plot or contrive (usually in a malicious sense)."

[3] *hagah*, "to murmur (in pleasure or anger); by implication to ponder, meditate, mourn, mutter, roar, talk."

[4] *Nicomachean Ethics*, fourth century B.C.

[5] "To Verify," *Leadership Journal*. 465 Gundersen Drive, Carol Stream, IL 60188.

[6] James S. Hewett, *Illustrations Unlimited* (Wheaton: Tyndale House Publishers, Inc., 1988), 486.

[7] Bacon, Francis. "On Revenge" (1625).

[8] Hewett, 486.

[9] Sydney J. Harris (1917–1986).

[10] Bacon, Francis. "On Revenge" (1625).

[11] Satires, c. A.D. 100. http://fordham.edu/halsall/ancient/asbook.html.

[12] Jacula Prudentum, 1651. Incidentally, this was also the motto of Gerald and Sara Murphy, the expatriate friends of F. Scott Fitzgerald who were the models for Dick and Nicole Diver in *Tender Is The Night*.

[13] Edwin Hubbel Chapin.

[14] *Leadership*, Vol. 4, no. 1.

[15] Anonymous. *Men of Integrity*, Vol. 1, no. 1.

[16] Gaylord Goertsen in *The Christian Leader* (February 26, 1991). *Christianity Today*, Vol. 35, no. 7.

[17] "The Parsonage®, Battle Plan Against Pornography," Sermon Outline, printed at http://family.org/ citing to http://enough.org).

[18] The Parsonage®, citing to Eric Schlosser, "The Business of Pornography," *U.S. News and World Reports* (2/10/1997).

[19] *Study by Adult Video News,* an adult industry trade magazine, and printed by Ralph Frammolino, and P. J. Huffstutter, "The Actress, the Producer, and Their Porn Revolution" *Los Angeles Times Magazine* (1/6/02).

[20] *Wall Street Journal*, November 26, 2001.

[21] Eric Schlosser, "The Business of Pornography," *US News and World Reports* (2/10/1997).

[22-23] Schlosser.

[24] For further information on U.S. business involvement in the pornography industry, see the *New York Times* article "Erotica, Inc.," by Timothy Egan (10/23/2000).

[25] Schlosser.

[26] "Alexa Research Finds 'Sex' Popular on the Web . . ." *Business Wire* (02/14/2001). [Note: The results were based upon a comprehensive two-year study by Alexa Research, a leading web intelligence and traffic measurement service.]

[27] *chamad*, "to delight in, covet, delectable thing."

[28] The word used here (*yester*) comes from the root *yatsar*, which means "to mould into a form; especially as a potter" and is one of the words used in Genesis 1 for God's work at creation. "The Hebrew word signifies not only the imagination, but also the purposes and desires" (*Treasury of Scripture Knowledge*).

[29] *Charash* literally means "to scratch, to engrave, to plough." Metaphorically, it means, from the use of tools, "to fabricate, to devise in a bad sense;" hence, from the idea of secrecy, "to be silent, to let alone;" hence by implication, "to be deaf (as an accompaniment of dumbness)."

[30] *spoudazo,* "to use speed, i.e. to make effort, be prompt or earnest:—do (give) diligence, be diligent (forward), endeavour, labour, study." This comes from the root *spoude,* which means, "speed," by implication "dispatch, eagerness, earnestness."

Chapter 10

[1] *sheqer,* "an untruth; by implication, a sham."

[2] *kazab,* "to lie (i.e. deceive); fail, (be found a, make a) liar, lie, lying, be in vain."

[3] *puwach,* "to puff, i.e. blow with the breath or air; hence to fan (as a breeze), to utter, to scoff."

[4] http://truthinjustice.org/peasley.htm. AP Newswire.

[5] William Barclay. *The Ten Commandments for Today. Timeless Truths for Today's Moral Issues,* (Grand Rapids: Eerdman's Publishing Co., 1973), 199–200.

[6] Barclay.

[7] In each seventh year the ground was supposed to lie fallow and the crops that did grow were not reaped; the trafficker in the seventh year produce was the man who failed to observe the law of Leviticus 25:1–7.

[8–9] Several of these points, and the discussion, are adapted from Barclay.

[10] Interestingly, this is the word from which "devil" is translated.

[11] Miguel de Cervantes (1547–1616) is also credited with saying, "A good name is better than great riches."

Chapter 11

[1] James S. Hewett, *Illustrations Unlimited,* (Wheaton: Tyndale House Publishers, Inc., 1988), 75.

[2] "Naughty" means "worthlessness; by extension destruction, wickedness." The naughty man is an unprofitable or worthless man before God because of the damage that he does to himself and his fellow men." "A froward mouth . . ." John Gill, in *John Gill's Exposition of Proverbs,* says of this word, "speaking perverse things, things contrary to the light of nature and reason, to law and Gospel." His words contradict and do not harmonize. These utterances tear down and do not edify.

[3] Thomas Lindberg, Stevens Point, Wisconsin. *Leadership,* Vol. 6, no. 4.

[4] This phrase is used at the beginning of nearly every New Testament epistle, and is also often found at the close.

[5] c. 445–365 B.C.

[6] *nirgan,* "from an unused root meaning to roll to pieces; a slanderer."

[7] This word means "without ceasing" and comes from a root (*ekteino*) "to stretch; to extend." The idea is that we "bend over backwards for each other, and we do it constantly."

[8] Adapted from: Arthur Lenehan, *The Best of Bits & Pieces,* (Economics Press, 1994).

[9] This is not to say that these things could not be made sinful. Some things are indifferent in one situation and wrong in another. Two examples are eating meat in this chapter and the washing of hands, pots, and pans in Matthew 15:1–9. It is not wrong to eat meat, but when one eats meat in honor of idols it becomes wrong (1 Corinthians 8:10–13). Alcohol may be an indifferent thing when used as a medicine (1 Timothy 5:23), but its use for intoxication is wrong (Proverbs 20:1; 23:29–33).

[10] http://quotedb.com/quotes/2751.

[11] Don Ratzlaff in *Christian Leader* (March 1993). *Christianity Today,* Vol. 37, no. 10.

Chapter 12

[1] Matthew Henry, *Commentary on the Whole Bible.* Vol. 3 (Hendrickson Publishers).

[2] "Unity" (various forms) is found an additional five times; the word "one" is found 1967 times.

[3] *Leadership,* Vol. 8, no. 4.

[4] *Leadership,* Vol. 11, no. 3

[5] James S. Hewett, *Illustrations Unlimited* (Wheaton: Tyndale House Publishers, Inc., 1988), 125.

[6] Robert C. Shannon, *1000 Windows*, (Cincinnati, Ohio: Standard Publishing Company, 1997).

[7] Anonymous, http://stcboston.org/broadside/11_2002/v60_no2_light.shtml.

[8] Hewett, 125–126.

[9] Bill Donahue, "The Church's Mission," *Seeds Tape Ministry*, Feb. 3, 1992.

[10] Haddon Robinson, "The Wisdom of Small Creatures," *Preaching Today*, Tape No. 93.

[11] McCoy, Marilyn. "Kids of the Kingdom." *Christian Reader*, Chester, Vermont.

[12] Fleury. *Hist. Eccles*. V. 2, p. 334.

Chapter 13

[1] Francis Brown, et. al., *Brown-Driver-Briggs Hebrew and English Lexicon*. (Hendrickson Publishers, Reprint edition, 1996).

[2] "Love," 33 times; "loveth," 9 times; "loved," 3 times.

[3] A. W. Tozer, *The Knowledge of the Holy* (San Francisco: Harper, 1961), 100–101.

[4] Jim Nicodem, "The Father Heart of God," http://SermonCentral.com/.

[5] This is the literal meaning of the phrase: "Sanctify [*hagiazo*, 'to make holy'] you wholly."

[6] Claudia Minden Weisz, "And God said, No," via Newsletter, nd, Lake Hills Church of Christ, 4519 Oak Hill Rd, Chattanooga, TN.

[7] Robert J. Morgan, *Nelson's Complete Book of Stories, Illustrations, & Quotes* (Thomas Nelson Publishers, 2000), 357.

[8] Michael Moss, "The Boy in the Well," Central Church of Christ Bulletin, Nashville, Tennessee, November 23, 2003.

[9] "full ended, that is, entire."

[10] Albert Barnes, *Barnes Notes on New Testament*, (Baker Grand Rapids: Electronic Version, E-Sword). Albert Barnes notes that this is strong language. It means to be fully and firmly persuaded or convinced. Paul was entirely convinced of the truth of what he said. It is the language of a man who had no doubt on the subject.

[11] *epitelesei*

[12] from *teros* (a watch; perhaps akin to G2334), "(ob-, pre-, re) serve, watch."

[13] *phulasso*, probably from G5443 through the idea of isolation.

Allen Webster is also the author of
more than 100 booklets and pamphlets
on a wide variety of Bible topics.
They are available at www.churchofChrist.info.

Place your order today!

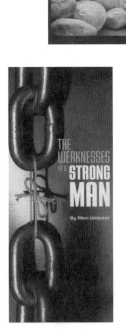

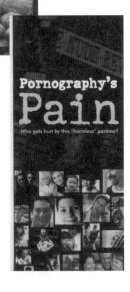